ACTIVATE YOUR ENGLISH

Intermediate Coursebook

**Barbara Sinclair
and Philip Prowse**

CAMBRIDGE UNIVERSITY PRESS

Published by the Press Syndicate of the University of Cambridge
The Pitt Building, Trumpington Street, Cambridge CB2 1RP
40 West 20th Street, New York, NY10011-4211, USA
10 Stamford Road, Oakleigh, Melbourne 3166, Australia

© Cambridge University Press 1996

First published 1996

Printed in Great Britain at
the University Press, Cambridge

ISBN 0 521 48420 0 Coursebook
ISBN 0 521 48419 7 Self-study Workbook
ISBN 0 521 48418 9 Teacher's Book
ISBN 0 521 48417 0 Class Cassette
ISBN 0 521 48416 2 Self-study Workbook Cassette
ISBN 0 521 48415 4 Self-study Workbook CD

INTRODUCTION

Welcome to *Activate Your English*, a short course at intermediate level. It will help you:

activate the English you have learnt but have forgotten

improve your knowledge of English vocabulary and grammar

feel more confident about understanding and using English in real life

find out more about how to learn English successfully.

The course consists of a Coursebook, a Self-study Workbook and a Self-study Workbook Cassette or CD. For the teacher there is a Teacher's Book and a Class Cassette.

Coursebook

This is for use in class, and has material for about 40 sessions (of between 45 and 60 minutes). The units have activities to help your speaking, listening, reading and writing skills, and to improve your vocabulary and grammar.

In each unit there is a section called 'It's your choice!' where you can choose activities you would like to do to practise your English. There are also 'Activate your grammar' sections to remind you of important grammar rules, and 'Activate your language' sections to help you remember useful vocabulary and expressions.

The course also helps you find out more about the way you learn English, so that you can be a better learner. 'Learning tips' throughout the course ask you to think about what you are learning and how you are learning.

There are four Review units which help you remember the language covered and evaluate your progress as you go through the course.

At the back of the book you will find a Grammar Review, which gives you more information about the grammar in the course, a list of irregular verbs, an Answer Key and Tapescripts for the listening exercises.

Self-study Workbook

This is for self-study outside class. It is very important because it offers 15–20 hours of further practice and revision of the language and skills covered in the Coursebook.

You will also need the Self-study Workbook Cassette or CD, which has listening and speaking practice activities for you to try on your own.

At the back of the Self-study Workbook you will find an Answer Key and Tapescripts.

We hope you enjoy activating your English!

Barbara Sinclair

Philip Prowse

Barbara Sinclair
Philip Prowse

MAP OF THE COURSEBOOK

Special note

Skills:
For details of skills contents, please see the individual units. The most important skill in the course is **speaking**, and this is practised in every unit. All units contain work on either reading or listening, or sometimes on both. There is a balance of skills work between the Coursebook and the Self-study Workbook, so that units that do not, for example, contain any listening work in the Coursebook will have it in the Self-study Workbook.

Pronunciation
The course focuses on pronunciation, stress and intonation in special practice activities in both the Coursebook and the Self-study Workbook.

Learner training
All units focus on practice in self-direction, and also activity evaluation and/or self-assessment. The map below focuses on other specific areas of learner training.

1

What do you say after 'hello'?

1
Languages, nationalities and music

a) Listen to these pieces of music. Number the list below to show the nationality of each piece of music.

American	Indonesian	British
Brazilian	South African	German
Egyptian	Argentinian	Russian

b) Listen to these people greeting each other on the beach in Rio de Janeiro. Number the list to show which languages they are speaking.

Arabic	Japanese	Italian
English	Chinese	Spanish
German	French	Portuguese

There are over 175 different nationalities in the world. Work in a group and make a list of as many nationalities as you can. Which group has the longest list? Identify the part of the world that each nationality comes from, using this list:

Africa	the Middle East	Asia
South America	North America	Europe
Australasia		

Can you pronounce the nationalities?

Learning tip

You can use a dictionary to check the pronunciation of words. In a dictionary the sound which is stressed in a word is usually shown by putting a small stroke before the sound.

Example
'Arabic, Argen'tinian.

Use a dictionary to check the stress for words describing nationality or a language.

2
How to be a Carioca

The people who live in Rio de Janeiro call themselves Cariocas. They say that a Carioca is someone who:

lives in the city of Rio, preferably on or close to the beach

says he or she is between 15 and 39 years old

usually goes to the beach before, after or instead of work

a) *How to be a Carioca* is a guide to Rio which tells you how or how not to behave. Read this extract about Carioca body language and try to remember as many details as possible. Close your book and tell another student how to be a Carioca.

b) How much of the extract do you believe? Make a note of the statements which may not be true and discuss them with a partner.

c) Body contact is different in different countries and cultures. What similarities and differences are there between Carioca behaviour and the behaviour of people in your country? Work with a partner and discuss:

shaking hands	kissing someone on the cheek (when? how often?)
touching someone's arms	
patting someone on the back	differences in behaviour between men and women
how close you stand to someone	

d) Make up sentences which are either true (T) or false (F) according to the text. Try out your sentences on another student.

Examples

You greet a Carioca by kissing her hand. F

Making eye contact is not essential.   T

Carioca Body Language

Body contact is essential. If you want to carry on a conversation like a true Carioca, stand as close as possible to the other person. Make body contact at least once for every sentence you say. Acceptable forms of body contact when talking to a Carioca are:

stroking his/her upper arm

tapping his/her shoulder or back

patting his/her cheeks

squeezing his/her hands

poking his chest

Body contact is most important when you greet another Carioca. Whether it's bumping into a friend on the street, joining a group of six for lunch, or walking into a party of twenty, it's essential that you make body contact with each person individually. It does not matter whether you know the person or not.

For example, you walk into a restaurant and notice a friend having dinner with a group of people. You have never seen any of the other people before. The following is the correct Carioca procedure for greeting your friend:

1 Say 'Oi' (oooo eeee) enthusiastically. Follow with 'Tudo bem?' (too doo 'bayn): 'Everything OK?'
2 Kiss your friend on both cheeks (the right cheek first, please).
3 Move around the table kissing each person present on both cheeks. Don't worry if that person has just taken a bite of his steak, or is deep in conversation with the person seated next to him.

Note: It is not necessary to make eye contact with other people, or say your name, or expect to hear theirs. As a general rule, women kiss women, women kiss men, and men kiss women. Men do not kiss men. The appropriate greeting between men is a handshake, followed by a few brisk, firm pats on the back with the left hand.

When you leave this group, do the following:

1 Return to your friend and say 'Tchau' (chow), which means 'Bye'.
2 Kiss your friend on both cheeks.
3 Move around the table kissing each person present on both cheeks. And remember: right cheek first!

e) Read through the text again and underline the gerunds.

Activate your grammar
Gerunds

The '-ing' form of the verb has two names: the present participle and the gerund. The present participle is used as a verb:

She's *kissing* him.
Acceptable forms of body contact when *talking* to a Carioca are ...

It can also introduce a clause:

Move around the table *kissing* each person present on both cheeks.

The gerund functions as a noun. It can be the subject or object of a sentence or come after a preposition:

Kissing the right cheek first is important. (subject)
In some countries hand-shaking replaces *kissing.* (object)
You greet someone by *kissing.* (after preposition)

➡ See Grammar Review 1 on page 81.

Activate your language
Greetings

In English the greeting 'How are you?' can have three different kinds of reply:

In normal health:	Fine/Very well, thank you. How are you?/ And you?
In poor health:	Well, not too bad/ Well, so-so. How are you?
Recovering from an illness:	Much better, thank you. How are you?

Note: 'How do you do?' is only said the first time you meet someone and the reply is the same - 'How do you do?'.

3
What can you talk about?

🔊 Listen to people's comments about what topics are suitable in different countries and what questions you can ask. Correct the following statements where necessary:

1 In south-west Nigeria it is polite to ask how many children someone has.

2 In Bangladesh be ready to tell people the exact age of your children in years, days and even hours.

3 In Vietnam it is OK to ask if someone is married.

4 In Nigeria it is always rude to ask how much someone earns.

5 In South Korea people like to know the age of someone they are talking to.

4
Making contact

a) You are flying to New York. You are sitting next to an American woman. She smiles and says 'Hello'. You say 'Hello'. There is silence. You want to continue the conversation, but you are not sure what to ask. Discuss which of the following topics you might choose to talk about.

The weather	Personal life: marriage	Name	Age
The flight		Salary	The news
Food	The time	Occupation	Politics
Borrowing something to read	The cost of items of clothing	The journey: where you're going	
	Family		

b) What questions might you ask about these topics?

Example
The weather: 'Isn't it a nice day?'

Make up questions for the topics which you think you could ask about.

c) Listen to an Englishman giving his view on topics for conversation. Tick the topics in (a) which he thinks are safe.

d) Make a list of things you would like to know about the other students in your class. Discuss the list with other students and make up questions for suitable topics. In a small group, ask your questions and answer other people's.

Activate your grammar
Question formation

1 'Yes/no' questions
Are you going to Rio?   **Do you live in Rio?**

2 'Wh-' questions
What's the weather like?   **Who's that?**

How old are you?   **When do we land?**

Where do you live?   **Which flight are you on?**

Why are we late?

3 Negative questions
Isn't it a nice day?

➡ See Grammar Review 2 on page 81.

5
It's your choice!
Personal information poster

Make a poster giving personal information about a real or imaginary person. First, decide on your own preferences, using the following checklist, and discuss your choices with other students and the teacher. Lay your poster out clearly.

I want to write:

☐ with others   ☐ alone

☐ about myself   ☐ about another person

☐ about real life   ☐ about something imaginary

☐ about facts (e.g. occupation, appearance, education)   ☐ about feelings (e.g. likes, dislikes, hopes, wishes)

6
Feedback: self-assessment

After this unit, how happy do you feel about using English to do the following?

	Happy	Not sure	Unhappy
Greet strangers			
Start a conversation with a stranger			
Say goodbye			
Ask for and give simple personal information			
Describe someone's nationality			

In this lesson how much have you learnt about the following?

	A lot	Something	A little
Differences in body contact between different countries			
Differences in topics of conversation between different countries			

In Self-study Workbook Unit 1
Grammar: gerund; vocabulary: occupations and places of work; intonation: questions; classroom English: question formation; your own test: dictation.

2 Ways of learning

1
Learning English

Close your eyes and think back to your first English lessons. Think of the classroom and the other students. Try to remember the sounds and the smell of the room. What is the teacher wearing? How are you feeling? What activities are you doing?

Work with a partner and tell each other about how you learnt English:

your age when you started

places: school, evening class, university, on your own?

number of hours a week

your feelings

the activities you did

2
Language learning aims

'I'm a fashion designer and I think English is important for my job. Now I think English is the second language in my country.'
Mei-Li, Taiwan

'I'm an electrical engineer. I use English because in my job I have to understand computers and everything is written in English. We cannot wait for translation into Spanish. I want to learn English because I need to communicate with people, not just for business.'
Carlos, Argentina

'I'm learning English for myself because I just like it and also for my profession.'
Giulia, Italy

Compare these students' aims with the aims of your class. Work in a small group and make a survey of class aims.

Why are students in your class learning English?

For business?

To pass exams?

For tourism?

In order to study in English?

To be able to read in English?

For other reasons?

3
Different language skills

a) Listen to some students of English talking about language skills. Study the chart and complete it with ticks where necessary to show which skills and language areas are important for the students. The chart is complete for the first student, Juan.

b) Complete the chart for yourself to show what is important for you. Compare results with a partner.

c) Use the chart to interview four other students about the skills and language areas they think are important for them.

Example
What language skills are important to you and why?

Report the results to the class.

Language skill	Juan	Angela	Yuko	Hiromi	Sven	Jacek	Yves	You
Vocabulary								
Grammar	✓							
Listening	✓							
Speaking	✓							
Reading								
Writing								
Pronunciation	✓							
Review								

4
What language learning type are you?

There are as many different ways of learning a language as there are language learners. However, it is possible to identify four main types. The purpose of this questionnaire is to help you identify which type you are most like and also to help you think about other ways of learning you might want to try.

a) Complete the green section.

b) Follow the instructions and complete either the red or the blue section.

c) Read the description of your type.

d) Then read the other three descriptions.

e) Do you agree with your result? Why? Why not? Form a small group with other students of the same type. Discuss the ways of language learning which suit you best. Tell the rest of the class about your conclusions.

WHAT LANGUAGE LEARNING TYPE ARE YOU?

1 Are you someone who
a) wants to know grammar rules?
b) doesn't worry about grammar?

2 When you are reading, do you usually
a) look up the exact meaning of new words?
b) work out roughly what a new word means?

3 When you are speaking, do you
a) use phrases you've learnt by heart?
b) try out new ways of saying things?

4 For you a word usually has
a) one clear meaning.
b) different meanings in different situations.

5 Are you more interested in
a) business English?
b) literature?

6 Are you more interested in
a) passing examinations?
b) being able to say what you want?

7 Do you listen more to
a) someone's exact words?
b) the sound of their voice?

If you chose more (a)s than (b)s, do the red questions.

If you chose more (b)s than (a)s, do the blue questions.

1 Do you choose the answers to questions
   a) rather carefully?
   b) without thinking a lot?

2 Do you
   a) always finish homework on time?
   b) sometimes finish homework late?

3 Do you feel better when you
   a) finish a piece of work?
   b) still have time to finish it?

4 Which is more important when studying,
   a) being organised?
   b) being able to change?

5 Are you more comfortable with activities which are
   a) clearly limited?
   b) open-ended?

6 When working with other learners, do you
   a) plan carefully before you start?
   b) decide what to do as you go along?

7 Do you like it more when
   a) the whole class does the same activity?
   b) you work in small groups?

If you chose more (a)s than (b)s, read 'The worker'.

If you chose more (b)s than (a)s, read 'The player'.

---

1 A mistake is when
   a) you break the rules.
   b) people don't understand you.

2 Do you judge users of English by
   a) how accurate they are?
   b) how well they express themselves?

3 When you listen, is it important to understand
   a) every word?
   b) what the speaker means?

4 When you are speaking, do you
   a) try and remember the rules?
   b) say what you feel?

5 Other people's mistakes
   a) should be corrected.
   b) are not important.

6 Which is more important,
   a) describing facts?
   b) expressing feelings?

7 The good language learner is someone who
   a) never makes mistakes.
   b) doesn't worry about making mistakes.

If you chose more (a)s than (b)s, read 'The thinker'.

If you chose more (b)s than (a)s, read 'The feeler'.

Activate your grammar
'Like' and 'would like'

The feeler is someone who likes reading.
The thinker is someone who would like to know everything there is to know.

'Like' can be followed by either a gerund or an infinitive with little change in meaning. 'Would like' has to be followed by an infinitive.

The following verbs can also be followed by either a gerund or an infinitive:

dislike   hate   prefer   love

However, 'enjoy' has to be followed by a gerund.

➡ See Grammar Review 3 on page 81.

The worker

The worker is someone who:

likes organisation and planning

enjoys doing exercises and drills

would like to work with the teacher all the time

has good study habits, is punctual and is good at homework

is comfortable with facts and routine

likes doing tests and being corrected

prefers writing to discussion or drama

dislikes doing project work

dislikes playing games or working in small groups

The player

The player is someone who:

likes being with people and enjoys variety and change

prefers listening and speaking to reading and writing

prefers playing games and working in groups to writing exercises

prefers competition and excitement to practice and homework

prefers trying lots of different activities to doing long projects

enjoys participating and performing

hates doing the same thing lesson after lesson

would like to do different things all the time

The thinker

The thinker is someone who:

wants to know why and is always looking for rules and principles

works independently and learns from individual study

enjoys listening to lectures and doing projects and longer written work

is very hard-working and always wants to get things right

prefers reading to taking part in discussions or group activities

likes getting feedback from the teacher

sometimes does not complete work and is often dissatisfied with it as it may not be perfect

would like to know everything there is to know

The feeler

The feeler is someone who:

is good at and enjoys learning languages

loves interacting and group and pair work

is interested in talking about emotions and personal topics

enjoys being with people and learns through co-operation

prefers taking part in discussions to studying rules and doing exercises

likes reading, roleplay and drama

is very sensitive to criticism and needs individual feedback

prefers speaking to writing

5
It's your choice!

The following activities are identified according to the four 'types' in the questionnaire. First, do the activity that fits with your 'type'. Then choose a different exercise to do (it is a good idea to try out the other activities, particularly if your questionnaire answers were evenly balanced).

After this, reflect on the questionnaire. What have you learnt about the type of learner you are and the sorts of activities that suit you best?

Worker: study plan

Work on your own or with another student to develop a study plan for the rest of the course. Consider these questions:

How many hours will you have in the classroom?

How much time each day/week can you give to private study outside the classroom?

When will your course end?

Then plan what you will do each day/week outside the classroom:

Vocabulary: How many words will you learn? Will you learn by topic (e.g. sport) or as you come across new words?

Reading: How many readers or other books will you read during the course?

Grammar: Will you use the Grammar Review section regularly?

Review: Will you go back over each unit one week and three weeks after you have completed it?

Player: vocabulary race

Join with other students for a vocabulary race. You need two teams and a referee. The rules are simple. The referee chooses a topic (e.g. clothes, music, work) and each team has one minute to write down as many words related to the topic as possible. The team with the most words wins. Then the referee chooses another topic.

Feeler: the good language learner

Work with other students to build up a psychological profile of the good language learner. Give her/him a name and imagine her/his family and home life. Think of all the qualities a good language learner needs. Then roleplay a dialogue between this person and someone who knows nothing about language learning.

Thinker: finding the rule

Look at these examples:

write – writing	complete – completing
be – being	sure – surely
true – truly	simple – simply
agree – agreement	

Work out a rule to say when the final 'e' of a word is dropped when a syllable is added. Check your rule in a grammar book or with your teacher and tell the rest of the class.

6
Feedback

Answer the following questions about Exercises 4 and 5 in this unit:

How do you feel about dividing the class into language learning types?

Are there some students who could be more than one type?

What have you learnt from these exercises?

Will you do the questionnaire again after a few more units?

In Self-study Workbook Unit 2
Grammar: 'like' and 'would like', defining; listening for the main points; pronunciation: silent letters; classroom English: grammar words; your own test: vocabulary topics.

3 My past

1
Where I grew up

a) Listen to seven people describing where they grew up. Number the drawings to show where each person lived.

b) Close your eyes and go back into the past. You are back in the place where you grew up. Open the front door and go in. Walk from room to room. What can you see and hear? What can you smell? How do you feel?

c) Work with a partner and describe where you grew up in as much detail as possible.

d) Think about your childhood. What things happened often or regularly? Think about your family and household routine. Tell your partner what you used to do.

Examples

My mother used to play with me.

My father used to cook.

We used to sit outside in the evenings.

Activate your language
Kinds of home

flat
apartment

detached/
semi-detached/
terraced house

bungalow

ground floor
first floor
second floor

attic
cellar

Activate your grammar
'Used to'

There was a big stove where my mother used to cook food and we used to sit together next to it.
You came into a corridor where my parents used to keep meat.

'Used to' describes situations or habits in the past which no longer happen or no longer exist. Negatives and questions are formed with the auxiliary verb 'did':

I didn't use to eat meat.
Where did you use to play?

Note: 'used' and 'use' are pronounced with /s/ not /z/.

See Grammar Review 4 on page 82.

Learning tip
Learning from others

More people speak English as a foreign language than as a mother tongue, so it is important to listen to lots of different ways of speaking. You can learn a lot of English from the other students in the class and by listening to foreign users of English. Don't worry, you won't 'learn' their mistakes! It is very likely that you will use English in the future to talk to someone whose mother tongue is not English, so it is good to practise now.

2
My life

Work with a partner and use the ideas below to tell each other about your life from birth until you left school.

My life
I was born on ... in ...
My mother's name was ...
and my father's name was ...
We lived at ...
The first thing I remember was ...
My favourite toy was ...
I used to ...

I went to primary school when I was ....
The school was ...
I wore ...
I felt ...
I enjoyed ...

When I was young there were some changes in my family.
... was born.
... died.
... got married.
... got divorced.

I went to secondary school when I was ...
The school was ...
I wore ...
My friends were ...
I was interested in ...
I enjoyed ...

I left school when I was ...
Then I ...
I felt ...

Activate your language
The family

mother	father
daughter	son
grandmother	grandfather
granddaughter	grandson
sister	brother
aunt	uncle
cousin	cousin
mother-in-law	father-in-law
daughter-in-law	son-in-law
sister-in-law	brother-in-law

Activate your grammar
Past simple: regular and irregular verbs

I went to primary school when I was seven.
My parents got divorced in 1982.

The past simple is used to talk about events or circumstances at a fixed point in time in the past. It is often used with time expressions (e.g. 'yesterday', 'last month/year', 'a day/week/ month/year ago') and with times, days and dates.

See Grammar Review 5 on page 82.

3
The things we've done

a) Work in a group of four or six. Ask each other about the first time you did things. Use this list and add more activities. When did you first:

drive a car?	fall in love?	have a cigarette?	make a long journey alone?
travel abroad?	kiss someone?	meet a foreigner?	

Examples

When I was 12.   Ten years ago.   I've never ...

Write a list about your group's activities.

Examples

Voula first had a cigarette when she was nine!

Abdul has never driven a car.

b) Ask questions to find out how many times the people in your group have done the following things. Take turns to ask the questions and note down the answers. How many times have you:

travelled abroad?	moved house?	been in love?	won money in a lottery?
been on television?	been in hospital?	been in a car accident?	bought a new car?
spoken to a speaker of English?	changed your job?		

Write a list showing what members of the group have done.

Examples

We've been on television twice.

We've moved house 16 times.

We've never won any money in a lottery.

Activate your grammar
Present perfect

I've been in love for ten years.
I've never had a cigarette.
I've bought a new car.

The present perfect tense links the past and the present. There are four main uses:

1 Something from the past which is still true now:
I've been in love for ten years.

2 Describing a period of time up to now:
I've never had a cigarette.

3 Stressing the present consequences of past actions:
I've bought a new car (and I've still got it).

4 A habit up until now or a repeated activity:
I've changed my job every three years.
I've been to Paris six times.

The present perfect is often used with the following time expressions:

just	already	before
ever	never	for
since		

➡ See Grammar Review 6 on page 82.

4
I'll never forget the day

Look at the titles and choose two passages to read. Tell another student about what you have read.

When I joined the Beatles

I'll never forget the day Brian Epstein called me up when I was working at a holiday camp and asked me to join the Beatles - it was a Wednesday in August 1962.
Ringo Starr

When I first visited England

On the boat from Calais to Dover: that was how I came to England the first time, from Kuwait. I was 16 and I had $20 in my pocket. For one and half years I washed dishes in the Grand Hotel in Eastbourne. Then I went home.
Khalid Ibrahim

When my first child was born

The nurse said 'Yes, you are the father of a boy.' I don't know what I did or said. I just gave a shout of excitement and rushed out, Leah and I were parents for the first time and of a son. I arrived home completely out of breath. My father and mother and my sisters were all there. How excited we were, and we gave thanks. And I think I walked just a little straighter, I held my head just a little taller and my step was just a little firmer.
Archbishop Desmond Tutu

When I got my first bicycle

It must be fifty years ago now but I'll never forget seeing the brand new bicycle sparkling outside in the sun. And then that first ride, with my father's hand ready to catch the back of the saddle if I fell. The smell of the rubber and leather and the swishing noise of the wheels on the road! I've travelled all over the world since then but I doubt if anything compares to the thrill I got when I saw my first bicycle.
Tony Hart

Adapted from *The Guardian* and *I'll Never Forget the Day* edited by B Willey

5
Interviews

Think about three or four important events in your life. The events can be very personal (like falling in love) or not (like passing an examination). Write down the names or dates of the events and give the paper to another student.

Interview your partner about one or more of the events and take notes. Questions could include:

| Can you tell me about the time you ... | What happened next? |
| Can you tell me what happened when you ... | And how did you feel? |

Form a small group and tell each other the results of the interviews.

6
It's your choice!

a) Choose an activity which suits your learning type.

Important dates

Make a list of important dates in your life. Next to each date write what happened and why it was important. Give as much detail as possible.

The famous person game

Work in one of two teams. Each team thinks of ten famous people. The teams take turns to describe a famous person without giving the name, and the other team has to guess who it is.

Pronouncing '-ed'

Why is '-ed' pronounced differently at the ends of past tense verbs? Think of 'pronounced', 'added' and 'happened'. Look at other verbs in this lesson. What is the rule?

Your creation

Work in a pair or small group to create an imaginary person who is very famous. Write down as many details as you can about the past life of this imaginary person.

b) Try another activity. What do you think now about the type of learner you are?

7
Feedback

Did you have any problems with this unit? What are you going to do to help yourself?

Activity	Problem	Solution
1		
2		
3		
4		
5		

In Self-study Workbook Unit 3
Grammar: present simple and past simple, 'used to', present perfect with 'ever/never/always', irregular verbs; pronunciation: '-ed' endings; classroom English: punctuation; your test: write in the verbs.

4 My future

1

What we're going to do - what the future will bring

a) Think about where you live. There are always jobs to be done: cleaning, tidying and buying new things, for example. Imagine you are going to spend all next weekend at home doing these jobs. Work with a partner and say what you're going to do.

Example
A: I'm going to sort out my clothes.
B: What else?
A: I'm going to clean the kitchen.

b) Fill in the thoughts of the second person in each cartoon, using these sentences:

a) She'll be lucky to sell a record!

b) I don't think we'll ever get there.

c) He'll probably lay an egg soon.

d) I think the sharks will be better company.

Activate your grammar

'Will' and 'going to' future

'Will' is used to forecast the future when we are fairly sure that something will happen, or to say what we want or expect to happen. It is often used after 'I think', 'I expect', 'I hope', and 'hopefully'.

Examples
Tomorrow's weather will be hot and sunny.
Hopefully in ten years' time I'll be a millionaire.

'Going to' joins the present and the future. It is used to forecast the future when there is evidence for it now, to express intentions, and to describe something that is about to happen.

Examples

It's going to rain.	(I can see the clouds.) Evidence now.
He's going to live in Italy.	(At the end of the summer.) Intention.
I'm going to be sick.	(I already feel bad.) About to happen.

➡ See Grammar Review 7 on page 82.

1 *Everything is going to work out fine!*

2 *You're going to be a STAR!*

3 *We're going to be late!*

4 *We're going to have such fun!*

c) Listen to this interview with a 19-year-old and number the statements to show the correct order.

Fly to South Africa	Visit Malawi	Live in Italy
Start university	Go to Zimbabwe	Travel to Zanzibar
Have a holiday in Malta	Get a job	

d) Listen to the interview again and read the tapescript, underlining the 'will' and 'going to' future.

2

Me in ten years

a) Read the questionnaire carefully and think about yourself in ten years' time. Let your mind go free and use your imagination. Think big – anything is possible in ten years' time! Make notes of your ideas.

b) Work with a partner and tell each other about yourselves in ten years' time.

c) Choose one section and write a short paragraph about it. Share your paragraph with the other students.

Activate your language

I expect/think/suppose/hope	I will ...
I wonder if / I'm not sure if	I will ...
What I'd really like is	to be ...
What I really want is	to be ...

Complete satisfaction!

Me in ten years

Relationship
- Will you have a partner (husband, wife or someone you live with)?
- What will your partner be like? What kind of personality will he/she have? What will he/she look like?

Health and fitness
- What weight will you be?
- How much exercise will you take? What kind of exercise?

Home
- What kind of home will you live in? A flat, a house, a tent, a caravan or a palace?
- What will your home look like? Describe it in as much detail as possible. Where will it be? How big will it be? What will you be able to see from the windows? How many rooms will there be? What kind of furniture will you have?

Work
- Will you have a job? If so, what will it be? Describe in detail the job you will have.

Money
- Will money be important to you?
- How much money will you need? How much money will you have?

Fun/relaxation
- What will you do for fun? What will your leisure activities be?

Creativity
- Will you write or sing or paint?
- Will you create a beautiful garden, cook wonderful meals or dance excitingly?

Friends
- Who will your friends be? Will they be important to you?
- What will you do with your friends?

Family
- Will you be close to your parents and family?
- Will you have children of your own?

Learning/self-development
- What will you want to learn?
- How will you develop?
- What new opportunities will there be?

Helping others
- How will you be able to help others? Will you do voluntary or charity work?

3
How long will you live?

a) Do this quiz and find out how long you will live. If you are a woman start with a total of 76 years. If you are a man start with a total of 69 years. Add or subtract years after each question.

b) How did you do? Discuss your results with the other students. Don't worry if you didn't get a high score. This quiz only gives a general idea. But perhaps it's worth looking at the areas where you 'lost' years and consider changing your lifestyle.

Learning tip

Many learners find it helpful to make a learning 'contract' with themselves. They write down what they are going to do to improve their English and when they are going to do it. Then they tick the 'Done' column when the activity is completed.

Activity	When	Done
Read a guided reader	Once a week	
Learn 10 new words	Every day	
Review last week's work	Every Sunday	
Listen to the radio news	Every morning	

1 Your age now

Are you under 40?
Add 2 years.

Are you 40 to 60 years old?
Add 3 years.

Are you aged 61 or over?
Add 4 years.

Age: _____

2 Where you live

Do you live in a large town or city?
Subtract 2 years.

Do you live in a small town or in the country?
Add 2 years.

Age: _____

3 Who you live with

Do you live alone?
Subtract 2 years.

Do you live with a partner or friend?
Add 3 years.

Age: _____

4 Education

Do you have a university degree?
Add 1 year.

Do you have a degree and further qualifications?
Add 2 years.

Age: _____

5 Activity

Do you work in an office?
Subtract 3 years.

Does your job keep you active?
Add 3 years.

Are you at home looking after children?
Add 1 year.

Do you take exercise for up to 30 minutes at least 3 times a week?
Add 2 years.

Age: _____

6 Your mood

Are you happy?
Add 1 year.

Are you unhappy?
Subtract 2 years.

Are you easy-going and relaxed?
Add 3 years.

Are you quick-tempered and aggressive?
Subtract 3 years.

Age: _____

7 Driving

Have you had any kind of road accident (even a small one) this year?
Subtract 1 year.

Age: _____

8 Bad habits

Do you smoke more than 40 cigarettes a day?
Subtract 8 years.

Do you smoke 20–40 cigarettes a day?
Subtract 6 years.

Do you smoke up to 10 cigarettes a day?
Subtract 3 years.

Do you drink the equivalent of a bottle of wine a day?
Subtract 1 year.

Age: _____

9 Your weight

Are you more than 20 kilos overweight?
Subtract 8 years.

Are you between 12 and 20 kilos overweight?
Subtract 4 years.

Are you between 5 and 12 kilos overweight?
Subtract 2 years.

Age: _____

10 Your health

Do you have an annual medical check-up?
Add 2 years.

Age: _____

11 Your family's health

Did any of your grandparents live to be 85 or older?
Add 2 years.

Did all four of your grandparents live to be 80 or older?
Add 6 years.

Did either of your parents die of a stroke or heart attack before reaching 50?
Subtract 4 years.

Did any of your close family (parents, brothers or sisters) develop cancer before they were 50?
Subtract 3 years.

Age: _____

4
Promises and aims

a) Work on your own and think about learning English. Think of two things:

something the other students can do to help you and give you confidence in class

something you can do to help the other students and give them confidence in class

b) In a small group share your ideas. Ask for promises from other students and give promises yourself.

Examples

I'd like to finish when I'm speaking. So please promise not to interrupt.

I promise not to come late and disturb the lesson.

c) Write down your long-term and short-term aims for learning English.

Examples

Long-term: By the end of this course I want to be able to . . .

Short-term: Therefore this week I will . . .

d) Share your aims with other students and find others with the same aims.

5
It's your choice!

a) Choose an activity.

Me in ten years' time

Write a personal poster describing your life in ten years' time. Use the headings from the questionnaire in Exercise 2 and include a plan showing how you will achieve these aims.

Survey

Work with a partner to do a survey of the other students. Ask what jobs they think they will have in ten years' time. Draw a chart to show the results.

The future

'I'll . . .'   'I'm going to . . .'

What are the differences? How many ways do you know of expressing the future in English?

A person in the future

Think of people you know (including public figures). What will their life be like in ten years' time? Choose one person and write a description of her/him in ten years.

b) Now try another activity. Which activity did you prefer? Why?

6
Feedback

What have you done in this unit?	
What have you learnt?	
What have you practised?	
What more would you like to do?	

In Self-study Workbook Unit 4
Grammar: 'will' and 'going to'; reading comprehension; pronunciation: the alphabet; classroom English: instructions and questions; your test: spelling.

REVIEW 1

A

Progress check

Do the following activities to check your progress.

1 Starting a conversation with a stranger

Work with a partner.

Partner A: Imagine you are in a plane flying from London to Los Angeles. You are travelling alone. The person sitting next to you looks very nice and you want to start a conversation. Introduce yourself and try to keep a conversation going for as long as possible.

Partner B: You are sitting next to A on the plane. Respond naturally.

When you have finished, Partner B should award points for Partner A's performance, as follows:

Score
Award up to 10 points for each of the following things:

Appropriacy: Was your partner polite? Did she/he choose suitable topics to discuss?

Accuracy: Was the language used correct?

Fluency: Did your partner speak spontaneously with few hesitations or repetitions?

Discuss and negotiate your scores with your partner.

Your score (out of 30): _____

If you scored 15 or less, look back at Exercise 3 in Unit 1 and then try again.

Swap roles and do the roleplay again.

2 Atsuko

Listen to Atsuko talking about why she needs to improve her English and say whether the statements below are true or false.

a) Atsuko's father thinks learning English will help her find a good husband.

b) Atsuko's father wants her to have an English husband.

c) Atsuko needs English for her job.

d) Atsuko has to travel abroad for her work.

e) Atsuko finds speaking English on the phone very hard.

f) Atsuko has to give presentations to customers in English.

g) Atsuko needs English to describe how telephone answering machines work.

h) Atsuko needs English for her holidays.

i) Atsuko has many English-speaking friends.

j) Atsuko's father doesn't know about her English boyfriend.

Score
Check your answers on page 87. Give yourself 2 points for each correct answer.

Total (out of 20): _____

3 Des'ree and Esther

Des'ree, 26, and Esther, 24, are sisters. Des'ree is a famous singer and Esther is studying for her MA in Psychology. Read the following text once only and then answer the questions on the next page.

Des'ree *We lived in South London until I was 12 and Esther was 10, and then Dad announced that we were to go and live in Barbados. He wanted us to learn about our culture. When we first arrived there I had a terrific nosebleed because of the heat and we both thought, Oh God, how are we going to survive this? Esther and I pretty much stuck together – we used to go to the beach every day, and to our uncle's farm, and we shared a bedroom right up until our late teens. It was good to be in a country where, suddenly, everyone looked the same as we did. And we were surrounded by black people who were doctors and lawyers, so we thought we could be anything we wanted to be. Growing up in the Caribbean gave us more spirit and drive.*

We used to listen to calypso and reggae, and to stories told to us by the older women in our family. We grew up surrounded by strong women who have always had to stand up for what they believe in, who were soft and gentle but didn't think that their place was in the kitchen – like Esther!

The hard part was when our parents split up and we had to come back to London. It was a tough time. Mum was a nurse and she used to work the day shift and then the night shift so she could give us the best. She sent us to a convent where we were sheltered from life back in Britain. Esther was much better academically than me.

Esther *When we were little in Barbados Des'ree and I used to sit all day in the huge mango tree at the bottom of our garden and share our secrets. We were both fans of Dallas on TV, and I remember Des'ree made up a song to the theme music. She sang it to all our friends and they thought it was wild. We always knew that Des'ree would be famous one day. She used to stand in the bedroom holding a pretend microphone, singing to the wallpaper. She saw every design in the wallpaper as a face, a member of her audience. I'm very protective and have always felt like the older one.*

Adapted from *The Sunday Times*

a) How did Des'ree and Esther feel on the day they arrived in Barbados?

b) What were the positive things about living in Barbados?

c) How did Esther know that Des'ree would be famous one day?

d) Did the sisters have a good relationship? How do you know?

How much of the text did you understand when you read it? Tick your answer.

☐ 1 90–100% ☐ 4 30–50%

☐ 2 75–90% ☐ 5 10–30%

☐ 3 50–75% ☐ 6 0–10%

Score
Check the answers to questions (a)–(d) on page 87. Give yourself up to 5 points per answer. Now add on the points for comprehension:

1: 5 points   4: 2 points

2: 4 points   5: 1 point

3: 3 points   6: 0 points

Total score (out of 25): _____

4 Just a minute!

Work with a partner and take turns to do this activity. Each person should talk for one minute on the following topic:

Me twenty years from now!

The partner who is listening should time the speaker with a watch.

Score
Up to 10 points for content

Up to 10 points for accuracy

Up to 10 points for fluency

Plus 5 bonus points for talking for a whole minute without stopping!

Total score (out of 35): _____

If you scored 17 or less, look back at Exercise 2 in Unit 4 and then try again.

5 Grammar check

Look at the following sentences. Some are correct and some have mistakes in them. Tick (✓) the sentences which are correct. Put a cross (✗) by the sentences which contain mistakes. Then try to correct the sentences with mistakes in.

a) Do you know what is the time?

b) How old are you?

c) You're going to Rio, isn't it?

d) Too much jogging is bad for your health.

e) What you think about this book?

f) I no need learn writing in English.

g) I don't have to speak English in my job.

h) Why do you learn English?

i) My mother used to played with me all day.

j) I use to sit in the mango tree.

k) I was born on 9th April.

l) I have been sick yesterday.

m) They have lived here since six years.

n) Have you ever been to Jamaica?

o) I'm going to Sweden on Tuesday.

p) Will it snow tomorrow?

q) I expect I become very rich one day.

r) I like to go to college next year.

s) What will your partner be like?

t) What would you like for your birthday?

Score
Check your answers on page 87. Score 1 point for each correct tick or cross. Score 2 points more for each corrected sentence.

Score: _____

Now add up your total score:

130–150	**Brilliant!**
110–129	**Good.**
90–109	**Satisfactory.**
70–89	**Not bad, but don't forget to review the units regularly.**
0–69	**You definitely need to review Units 1–4 again.**

B
Checklist

Use this checklist to record how you feel about your progress. Tick if you are satisfied with your progress. Put a cross if you are not satisfied.

I can	yes/no
introduce myself	
talk about myself	
start a conversation and keep it going	
talk about my language learning aims	
say what I need and have to do	
describe my childhood	
talk about important events in the past	
talk about my hopes and desires	
talk about my plans and intentions	

I know	yes/no
some useful expressions and topics for polite conversation	
more about my language learning needs	
more about my learning style	
about body language in different cultures	
how to use a dictionary to check the stress and pronunciation of a word	
a lot about the people in the class	
how well I'm doing	

C
Personal plan

What problems do you have and how do you plan to help yourself?

Problems

_____

Plans

_____

_____

5 Family life

Speaking
Discussing families and family problems; giving advice.

Grammar
Simple and first conditionals.

Vocabulary
Verbs to express ways of speaking.

Listening
Listening to a radio broadcast.

Reading
Reading a newspaper article for enjoyment and understanding.

Learner training
Practice in self-direction; self-assessment.

1
Our families

a) Work together to find out about each other's family relationships. Work out how many students fit into each of these categories and write the total in the box.

☐ the oldest child in the family   ☐ the youngest child

☐ a middle child   ☐ an only child

☐ most like their mother   ☐ most like their father

☐ married or live with partner   ☐ live with friends

☐ live with parents   ☐ live with other relatives

☐ live alone

b) How has your place in the family affected your life? Join other students to make these groups:

Oldest child   Youngest child   Middle child   Only child

What experiences do you have in common?

c) Discuss with other students:

What makes a family?

Why do different people have different ideas about families?

G. GOODMAN   MARGATE

2
Treasure

a) What problems do parents and teenage children have? What topics cause arguments?

b) Describe the girl in the pictures. How old is she? What are her interests? Imagine that this girl is your daughter. What problems do you have with her?

c) The text is called 'Dial M for Murder by Mother'. What do you think it is about? The girl in the pictures is called Treasure. Why do you think her mother calls her this name? Read to see if you were correct.

Dial M for Murder by Mother

Our telephone bill is £325. I do not find this amusing. Treasure apparently does. She finds the whole thing hugely entertaining. She ignores repeated requests and reasonable arguments to limit usage, and when I finally approach, maddened, screaming hoarsely, 'Get off the phone!' she just smiles into the phone.

Treasure will risk anything to use the phone. Returning home from even the briefest trip, she will rush to it, grab it and hold it on her knee. 'Who can I phone?' she asks, staring wildly into the air. She strokes its little plastic body. 'I'll phone Lizzie,' she cries. 'No, you won't,' I reply. 'It isn't six yet.'

'I must. I've got to.' She waits until six. She cannot rest, work or eat. She walks around the house, watching the clock, waiting, hoping someone will ring. At six she ties herself to the telephone, talking and laughing fiercely. I could hear every top-volume word from the bottom of the garden but Treasure is determined I shall not listen.

'Shut the door,' she roars bossily as I leave the room. I refuse. I am carrying a mountain of dirty cups, plates, banana and orange skins, and chewed yoghurt pots which she

and the dog have left. I haven't a free hand. I don't really want the door shut anyway. Once it's shut the dog cannot get in or out freely and starts to bark and scratch, and when Treasure is on the phone she is unable to move and help the dog. It can scratch its claws off and bark

itself dumb, and Treasure will not move a muscle. I am forced to return on such occasions and let it out myself.

'Why didn't you open the door?' I snap. 'I didn't hear,' says Treasure, looking hurt. 'Really I didn't.' But she can hear the telephone even on the quietest ring and hidden under the duvet on my bed. Someone phones at 10pm, Treasure's supposed bedtime. 'She's asleep,' I growl. But she has heard its tiny ring. She crawls exhaustedly from her bed. 'Who was it?' she croaks. She cannot sleep without this knowledge. She cannot sleep with it. She will lie awake wondering what she has missed and planning tomorrow's return call.

I just don't know what to do. 'Get Treasure her own phone,' my friends say, 'but for incoming calls only.' Then they can all phone her on that and at least my line will be clear. All I'll have to worry about is when, behind her closed bedroom door, glued to her telephone, will Treasure ever do her homework and go to sleep? 'She's only copying you,' my friends say. 'What do you do when you're upset? You run to the phone and tell everyone.' So it's my fault again!

From *The Guardian* (abridged)

---

d) The text has six paragraphs. Number the paragraphs and match them with these topics:

The sound of the phone	Waiting to make a call	Having to make a call
Laughing at mother	Solving the problem	Closing the door

e) Vocabulary: speech verbs
Find verbs in the text which describe ways of speaking. The first one has been done for you.

Verb	Way of speaking
1 scream	shout very loudly
2 c _____	shout loudly
3 r _____	sound like a lion
4 b _____	sound like a dog
5 s _____	speak quickly and sharply
6 g _____	sound like an angry dog
7 c _____	sound like a frog

Activate your grammar
Pronoun 'it'

We use words like 'it' to refer back to information we already know. For example, in the second paragraph Treasure's mother writes: 'she will rush to it, grab it and hold it on her knee'. Here 'it' refers to the phone.

f) What is referred to in these sentences?

1 She strokes **its** little plastic body (paragraph 2)

2 Once **it**'s shut (paragraph 4)

3 let **it** out myself (paragraph 4)

4 Who was **it**? (paragraph 5)

5 She cannot sleep with **it** (paragraph 5)

g) Work with a partner and roleplay the situation between Treasure and her mother. Treasure is talking on the phone to a friend. Begin:

Mother: Get off the phone.

Treasure: She wants me to get off the phone.

h) How about your own family? What were relations like between you and your parents when you were a teenager? If you have children of your own, do you find anything familiar in the relationship between Treasure and her mother?

3

Divorce and you

a) This girl's parents are splitting up – they're getting divorced. How do you think she feels? What is she thinking?

 b) What advice can you give the girl? Discuss this with another student and then listen to an extract from a radio programme called 'Divorce and You'.

 c) Was your advice the same as the advice given on the radio? Listen again to the extract, which is in four sections. Pause after each section and make notes.

Your feelings	
Ways of getting help	
Seeing your other parent	
New partners	

Look at the tapescript on page 91 to check your notes.

 d) Listen again and complete these sentences.

1 If you're so upset that it's affecting your school work, friendship or hobbies . . .

2 People can only help if . . .

3 But if you ask them questions and let them know you need to talk, . . .

4 You may be worried that it will upset the parent you live with . . .

e) Roleplay the conversation between a child whose parents are splitting up and an adult – a teacher or family friend.

Photo posed by model

Activate your grammar

Simple and first conditionals

If you are upset, it is best to tell someone.
People can only help if you let them know something is happening.
If you ask them questions, they will usually try to help.

a) Simple conditional

'If' clause	Main clause
If you are upset	**it is best to tell someone.**
'if' + present simple	*present simple*

This form is often used to express a general truth. It means that one thing always follows from another.

b) First conditional

'If' clause	Main clause
If you ask them questions	**they will usually try to help.**
'if' + present simple	*'will' + infinitive without 'to'*

This form is used to talk about possibilities now and in the future. What will happen is not certain but it is possible.

➡ **See Grammar Review 8 on page 82.**

4

Quiz: family and marriage

Which of these statements are true and which are false?

1 ☐ In Sweden and Iceland more than half the children are born outside marriage.

2 ☐ In Greece only one child in 50 is born outside marriage.

3 ☐ For every two marriages in Britain there is one divorce.

4 ☐ The average age for marriage in Europe is 27 for men and 24 for women.

5 ☐ The European countries with the highest numbers of one-parent families are Ireland, Britain and Italy.

6 ☐ In Britain more than a quarter of households are made up of one person living alone – twice as many as 30 years ago.

7 ☐ Women have more children in Ireland than anywhere else in Europe.

8 ☐ Britain has the second-highest marriage rate in Europe.

9 ☐ One third of all the world's households are headed by single parents – 90 per cent of them women.

10 ☐ The average age at which a woman has her first child in Britain is 27.5; 20 years ago it was 24.

5

It's your choice!

Choose the activity which you find most interesting
or useful.

Family history

Make a family tree for yourself. Include as many
people as you like. Discuss your family tree with
another student who has also made one. Are the
trees similar? Is the size of your family usual in your
country?

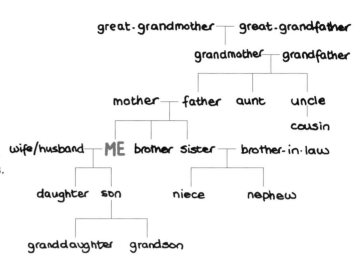

Feelings

Re-read the tapescript for Exercise 3 and make a list
of all the adjectives used to describe negative feelings.
For each one, can you find other adjectives which
have similar meanings?

Make a similar list of adjectives to describe positive
feelings.

Treasure

Work in a small group and create chain stories about
Treasure. To make a chain story one student starts
with a sentence, then the next student continues the
story with a sentence, and so on. Use these situations:

Treasure and . . .

food	guests	parties
cleaning	clothing	holidays

Letter writing

Imagine that you are Treasure. Write a letter to a
friend living abroad, describing your life at home and
saying how you feel.

6

Feedback

How much do you agree or disagree with these statements? Mark them
according to this scale:

5 – Strongly agree   3 – Neutral/Don't   1 – Strongly disagree
                  know

4 – Agree   2 – Disagree

a) I don't like talking about family and personal matters in class.

b) I enjoyed reading about Treasure.

c) The listening 'Divorce and You' was difficult.

d) I enjoyed doing the quiz.

e) I prefer to do all the 'It's your choice!' activities, not just one.

Write the letters (a) to (e) on a piece of paper with the number you chose
beside each one and give the paper to your teacher. Do not put your name
on the paper. The teacher will tell you the result of the feedback.

In Self-study
Workbook Unit 5
Grammar: simple and
first conditionals; learner
training: appropriacy;
vocabulary: sounds;
pronunciation; classroom
English: saying you
don't follow; your test:
oral test.

6 My profile

Speaking
Describing character, personality and beliefs.

Grammar
Pointer words: 'this' and 'that'.

Vocabulary
Character adjectives.

Reading
Reading a magazine article for detail.

Learner training
Word networks; practice in self-direction; activity evaluation.

1
Famous people

a) Who are the people in the photographs? What do you know about them?

b) Work with a partner. Choose the name of a famous person (dead or alive) and write it on a small piece of paper or a sticky label. Stick or pin the paper on to your partner's back without showing or saying the name.

Ask each other yes/no questions to find out who you are. Make up answers if you are not sure.

Examples

Am I alive now?	No.
Was I a woman?	Yes.

c) Take off your label but keep your identity as the famous person. Imagine you are at a party. Walk around and introduce yourself to the other famous people at the party. Answer questions about yourself.

d) Work in a pair. One partner is a famous person, the other a journalist. The journalist interviews the famous person.

1

2

3

4

2
Helen Sharman

a) Word association: Before reading the text, work in a small group. One student calls out the following words and the others say the first words they think of.

space travel   astronaut   rocket

b) Who is Helen Sharman? Look at the photograph and the first paragraph of the text.

c) Read the text.

An interview with Helen Sharman

Thirty-five years after the first manned space flight, Britain has produced just one astronaut, a Sheffield woman called Helen Sharman, who was 27 years old when the Russians shot her into space in 1991. She had been chosen out of 13,000 who replied to the original 'Astronaut Wanted' advertisement. She was a woman. She was not bad looking. She worked as a research scientist for Mars chocolate. All this made for easy headlines.

Now she has written her autobiography, *Seize the Moment*. 'I grew up in an ordinary background that will be familiar to hundreds of thousands of British people,' the book begins. 'In every street you'll find someone like me.'

'And being in space you look back on the Earth and you haven't got your hi-fi in the space craft, your washing machine or your microwave. You don't need them. You don't really miss them.'

People, she says, are naturally fascinated by space travel, not only because of its relation to the mystery of where we come from, but because they suspect it reveals things about human nature. What had she learnt? 'Simple things really. Living in Russia showed me what was important. Before, I was on a reasonable salary. I was single, no dependants, and I wanted to earn more money, because I wanted to own a bigger flat and a faster car. That was what my life was about. I went to Russia and people there didn't have flats or cars. So they didn't aspire to bigger or faster ones. What they had was family and friends. That was what was important to them.

'And being in space you look back on the Earth and you haven't got your hi-fi in the space craft, your washing machine or your microwave. You don't need them. You don't really miss them. The things we would actually talk about were our family and our friends, and that confirmed to me what was important in life. To me now, money is not important - but I know that without people my life wouldn't zing any more.'

How did she vote in the last election? 'That is not a subject for this interview.' Does she believe in God? 'There's no proof to me that there is a God and no proof to me that there isn't, so I have to keep an open mind. Being in space didn't make me necessarily think somebody must have created all this. It's there, so maybe somebody did or it may just be there.'

'Modern astronauts are all very much like I am,' she says, 'all chosen to be able to fit into a team. We need to be reasonably laid-back about life, with a reasonable sense of humour and to be fairly hard-working in order to get through the training. We are not like the early astronauts who were jet fighter pilots. They had to be very brave, and they were often going up alone. I was given a wonderful opportunity, but I was just one of a number of very ordinary people who had this wonderful opportunity.'

From *The Observer Magazine* (abridged)

d) Read this description of Helen Sharman and underline the parts which are not true.

Helen was born in 1954. She became Britain's first and only astronaut. Now someone has written a book about her. The book describes her unusual childhood and family background. Helen believes that people are interested in space travel because they want to know how the world began. She went to live in Russia because she wanted a bigger flat and a faster car. However, she found that although Russian families were larger, their flats were not. Money used to be important for her but it is no longer. Helen believes in God and votes conservative. The first astronauts had to be very brave. But now anyone can become an astronaut if they are hard-working enough.

e) What did Helen learn about money and possessions? What does she think about God? Do you agree with her? She describes herself as an ordinary person. Is she?

3
Vocabulary

a) Find words in the text which have the following meanings:

1 surroundings (paragraph 2)

2 well-known (paragraph 2)

3 very interested (paragraph 3)

4 uncovers (paragraph 3)

5 unmarried (paragraph 3)

6 people who rely on you (paragraph 3)

7 aim to have (paragraph 3)

8 be exciting (paragraph 4, colloquial word)

9 relaxed (paragraph 6)

10 courageous (paragraph 6)

b) Make up a title for the text.

c) Which of the following adjectives best describe Helen?

matter-of-fact	intelligent	romantic
boring	daring	hard-working
thoughtful	sensible	straightforward
careless	exciting	open-minded
ambitious	realistic	relaxed

d) Look back at the interview. The first paragraph ends with 'All this made for easy headlines.' The word 'this' refers back to the four previous sentences, from 'She had been chosen ...' to 'Mars chocolate'. What do the following words refer to in the text?

1 '**That** was what my life was about' (paragraph 3)

2 '**That** was what was important to them' (paragraph 3)

3 'You don't really miss **them**' (paragraph 4)

4 '**That** is not a subject for this interview' (paragraph 5)

5 '**It**'s there' (paragraph 5)

Activate your grammar
Pointer words: 'this' and 'that'

'This' and 'that' can be used to refer backwards to something mentioned earlier. 'This' can also be used to refer forwards to something which will be mentioned.

Examples
This is what I said. (forwards or backwards)

That is what I said. (backwards only)

➡ **See Grammar Review 9 on page 83.**

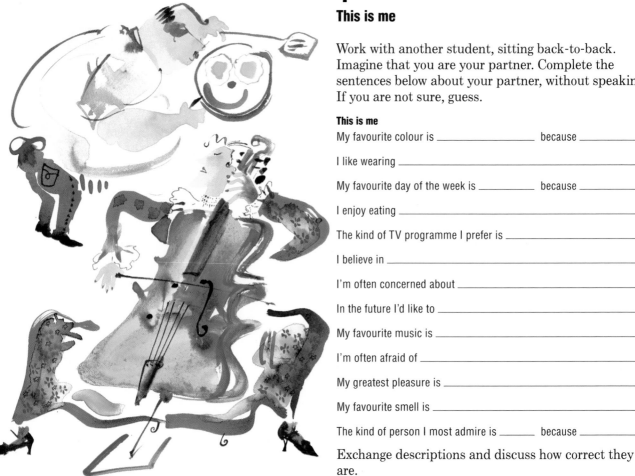

4
This is me

Work with another student, sitting back-to-back. Imagine that you are your partner. Complete the sentences below about your partner, without speaking. If you are not sure, guess.

This is me

My favourite colour is _____ because _____ .

I like wearing _____ .

My favourite day of the week is _____ because _____ .

I enjoy eating _____ .

The kind of TV programme I prefer is _____ .

I believe in _____ .

I'm often concerned about _____ .

In the future I'd like to _____ .

My favourite music is _____ .

I'm often afraid of _____ .

My greatest pleasure is _____ .

My favourite smell is _____ .

The kind of person I most admire is _____ because _____ .

Exchange descriptions and discuss how correct they are.

5
Vocabulary development

Try out a word network as described in the learning tip. Use the topic 'Space travel', or choose a different topic of your own.

Learning tip

Word networks are a useful way of remembering and developing vocabulary. Choose a topic and write it in the middle of a sheet of paper. Close your eyes and think of the topic. What words come to your mind about the topic? Write them on the paper and join them to the topic with lines. (If you think of a word in your own language and don't know it in English, look it up in a dictionary.)

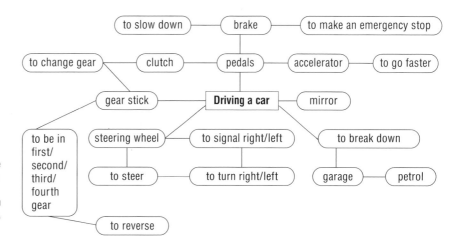

6
It's your choice!

a) Choose an activity.

Job application

Write a brief description of yourself to use when applying for a job. Use these headings:

Name

Address

Date of birth

Phone number

Qualifications (details of your education and the examinations you passed)

Experience (a list of the jobs you have had, starting with now and going back to the past. Give dates and a one-sentence description of each job.)

Liar

Find out or make up strange facts about famous people or people you know. Some of the 'facts' must be true, others false. Play a game of 'Liar' with another student who has to guess which are true.

Examples

1 Picasso's real name was Pablo Diego José Francisco de Paula Juan Nepomuceno Crispin Crispiano de la Santísima Trinidad Ruiz y Picasso.

2 Mrs Thatcher only sleeps for four hours a night.

3 Gerald Ford was the only American President to have been a male model.

4 Fidel Castro used to work as a film extra in Hollywood.

5 The first woman in space was Valentina Tereshkova in 1983.

Brain teasers

1 Brain teasers are puzzles which make you think.

Example

```
  R
R O A D  = crossroads
  A
  D
```

Can you work out these brain teasers?

a) S̲T̲AND   b) DEATH LIFE
   I

Do you know any other brain teasers?

2 Anagrams are words made up of the letters of other words.

Example

night   thing

Can you solve these anagrams, which are words from this unit?

mean   saw   taps

slit   won   lame

Make up some more anagrams.

Celebrity

Think of a character in a book or film. Work with another student and either write or roleplay an interview with the character.

b) Talk to students who did the activities you did not choose. Ask them what they thought of the activities and do the one which sounds best.

7
Feedback

Work in a group and take it in turns to give your views on the following topic:

The English classes so far: one thing I like and one thing which could be better

Each group member has a turn to speak without being interrupted. If you don't have a firm opinion on the topic or if you don't want to speak, just say 'Pass'.

In Self-study Workbook Unit 6
Reading and listening: two poems; grammar: articles; vocabulary: compound adjectives, adjective suffixes '-less', '-ful'; pronunciation: silent letters; classroom English: asking for help; your test: jumbled sentences.

7 Some good advice

1

Young people are getting worse …

Discussion points:

a) People say that young people are more badly behaved than before. What do you think?

b) Is the problem worse in some countries than others? Why? What about your country?

c) If your teenage son or daughter had behaviour problems, who would you go to for advice? Why?

2

Kevin

a) Read about Kevin, a 15-year-old British teenager living in Coventry. What are his problems? Why do you think he has them?

MONTGOMERY SCHOOL

13th May, 1996

Dear Mr and Mrs. Blair,

Further to my last letter dated 9th March and our telephone conversation of last week, I am writing to ask you both to come to a meeting at the school so that we can discuss what to do about Kevin's behaviour. He has missed at least 50 per cent of his classes in the last month and does not do his homework. He is rude to his teachers and classmates. On Friday he was found spraying graffiti on the school wall. He has also been seen by members of the staff in a local pub.

We need to discuss your son's behaviour urgently. Please telephone my secretary to arrange a time for a meeting next week. It would be most convenient if you could come after 4.30 pm and it would be useful if Kevin joined us for the meeting.

I very much hope that we can help Kevin in this way.

Yours sincerely,

Doris Williams
Principal

b) Now listen to Kevin. What else do you know about his problems? What do you think he should do? Tick your answers below.

Kevin should:

- [ ] obey his parents
- [ ] stay on at school and study hard
- [ ] leave school at 16 and try to find a job somewhere
- [ ] leave home and stand on his own feet
- [ ] join the armed forces
- [ ] see a counsellor
- [ ] try talking to his parents more
- [ ] be suspended from school
- [ ] be punished
- [ ] do something else. What?

c) What are your reasons for these answers? Compare and discuss your ideas with a partner.

3
Informal language

In the sentence on the left, Kevin uses a formal expression. On the right are some of his informal expressions which have a similar meaning.

Formal	Informal
They criticise everything I do.	They go on at me all the time.
	They nag me all the time.
	They're always getting at me.
	They say everything I do is rubbish.

Use your dictionary to find the formal expressions or meanings for these informal ones:

Expressions with 'get'

1 Stay calm. Don't let it get to you.
2 You really don't get it do you? I said, 'No!'.
3 What are you getting at?
4 We got off on the wrong foot, didn't we?
5 Mmmm, I really get off on chocolate ice-cream!
6 He got off with my friend at the club last night.
7 It's hard, but you'll get over it one day.
8 Let's get cracking!
9 Time is getting on.
10 We got on to the police immediately.

Expressions with 'go'

1 I'm going all out for promotion this year.
2 He didn't go along with the plan.
3 She went back on her promise.
4 This will go down as the most exciting match this year!
5 It was touch and go for a while.
6 He went for him with a knife.
7 It's personal. I don't want to go into it now.
8 I'm going bananas!

Do you know any more expressions with 'go' and 'get'? Which expressions do you want to learn?

4
Asking for and giving advice

Below are five pieces of advice. Listen to the three people asking for advice and choose the best suggestion for each. Say why you think it's the best advice.

a) Have you ever thought about buying your own house?

b) If I were you, I'd show her a photo of an unattractive woman and tell her it's your secretary.

c) Well, I think you should explain that you had no choice. You had to do it because of your mother's honour.

d) I'd go to the police. You can't let that happen again.

e) I'll tell you what I would do. I'd get a baby-sitter and be out one evening when he comes home. Let him get his own dinner.

f) I'd leave home if I were you.

5
What's your advice?

a) Imagine you are talking to the following people who are asking for your advice about Kevin. What advice would you give about Kevin's problems?

1 Kevin's school principal

2 Kevin's parents

3 Kevin

b) Now roleplay your conversations with a partner. Take it in turns to be the people listed above.

6
A dangerous world?

Discussion: Is the world a more dangerous place than it used to be? If so, how? Why?

If you could make the laws in your country, what would you do about:

murderers?	rapists?
car thieves?	child molesters?
burglars?	drug dealers?
football hooligans?	pet snatchers?
people who make racist attacks?	

7
It's your choice!
Forum: discussion game

Work in a small group. Think of three problems, write them on separate pieces of paper and fold them up. Don't let the other members of your group see them. Collect all the folded pieces of paper in a box. Take it in turns to choose a piece of paper and read out the problem to the group. Each person in turn should give some advice. Each good piece of advice gets one point. The person who makes the most successful suggestions gets the most points. Continue until all the problems have been read out.

Survey: speaking and writing

Devise a questionnaire to find out what people would do about a particular problem in society today. Try the questionnaire on some people in your class.

Kevin: writing

Imagine you are Kevin. The counsellor has asked you to write a journal for a day to help you to think about how you feel and why.

Grammar: investigating and writing

Use a selection of grammar books to help you find out about the second conditional in English. What forms can it take? How is it used? How is it different from first and third conditionals?

Take notes and then write a 'Second conditional fact sheet' for the others in your class.

8
Feedback

Did you have any problems with the activities in this unit? If so, what? What should you do about them?

Activity	Problem	I should
1		
2		
3		
4		
5		
6		
7		

In Self-study
Workbook Unit 7
Grammar: practice in second conditional; vocabulary: informal expressions with 'put'; reading comprehension; your own test: formal/ informal puzzle.

8 Guess what happened next!

1
Good news

Tell another student about something which made you feel good yesterday, last week and last year. You might think about:

a success at work   passing an examination   meeting someone new   a family event

2
True confessions

True Confessions is a popular radio programme. People phone in and confess to practical jokes and tricks they have played on other people.

First caller

 a) The first caller tells a story which takes place in a supermarket. Before listening, discuss what the story may be about. Listen to the cassette to find out if you were right.

b) Listen again and take notes. Then retell the story from the point of view of the old lady. She is telling a police officer what happened.

c) The story begins 'When I was living …'. 'I was living' is an example of the past progressive tense. Listen again while looking at the tapescript and note down other verbs in the past progressive tense.

Activate your grammar

Past progressive

When I was living in Manchester I worked in an office.
The manager was standing in the supermarket doorway when the trolley hit him.

The past progressive refers to a past event or situation which had started but not finished. It is often used to describe the background when we tell stories.

The trolley hit him

The manager was standing in the doorway

➡ **See Grammar Review 11 on page 83.**

Learning tip

'Listening' (1)

Here are some ideas for improving your listening:

1 **Try closing your eyes while listening to the cassette. Imagine you can see a picture of what you are hearing.**

2 **Listen actively. For example, you know from the drawing that the first story is about a supermarket so you can expect that it will contain words to do with shopping.**

3 **Listen for 'connectors' like 'then', 'next', 'after that' which help structure your listening.**

4 **Don't panic if you miss a few words. Concentrate on getting the general meaning.**

5 **Don't worry if you didn't get everything the first time. Ask for repetition or play the recording again.**

Second caller

a) The second story is told by a woman, and is about a trick she played on her boyfriend. Before listening, try to guess what she did.

b) Listen and mark the sentences true or false.

1 It happened in Scotland.

2 Ralph was very attractive.

3 He was going to marry Kathy.

4 Kathy worked in a sports shop.

5 Kathy and Ralph went to Australia together.

6 Ralph went to America alone.

7 Kathy bought a mouse.

8 Ralph sold the house.

c) In the story the woman says: 'I *had met* my dream man'. Listen again while looking at the tapescript and note down more examples of the past perfect tense.

Activate your grammar

Past perfect

This was when I was 19 and had met my dream man.
He had lied to me and had taken someone else.

The past perfect tense is used when we are talking about a past event and want to refer to something which happened even earlier in the past.

I had met dream man	I was 19 years old	
Before time of story	Time of story	Now

➡ **See Grammar Review 12 on page 83.**

Learning tip

Listening (2)

Listening is a relaxing way of learning and the more you listen, the more you'll learn. Study these ways of listening and choose the one(s) you like the best.

1 **Get the recordings of some readers and listen to them while you read. This will improve your reading speed and pronunciation.**

2 **Tune your car radio to an English-speaking station. You don't need to concentrate on the exact meaning – just let the language wash over you as you drive.**

3 **On your way from one place to another, use your walkman to listen to stories or songs.**

4 **Share cassettes with other students. You don't have to buy pre-recorded cassettes – you can make your own recordings by reading stories on to a cassette or asking an English speaker to do so.**

5 **You can record radio or TV broadcasts, but it is worth checking to find out whether it is against the law to do this in your country.**

6 **If you are going to listen to the news in English on radio or TV, it's a good idea to have a quick look first at a newspaper in your own language, so that you are familiar with the news topics.**

3
Keeping a conversation going

In both stories the radio presenter encourages the speakers to continue. For example, in the first story he says: 'What happened then?'.

Look at the tapescripts again, and note down the words the presenter uses to encourage the speakers to continue. Compare notes with another student.

Activate your language
Telling a story

1 Starting
Have you heard the story about …?
Did you hear about …? No? Well, …
Did you see in the paper/hear on the radio that …?

2 Keeping going
You'll never guess what happened next.
Do you know what? Then …

3 Ending
So that's what happened.
That's how it ended.

4 Showing that you are listening
I see.   Uh-huh.
Yes.   Oh!
Really?

5 Asking someone to continue
Do go on.   What happened next?

6 Asking for repetition
I beg your pardon?
Could you say that again, please?
Could you repeat that please?

7 Checking
Did you say that …?
Do you mean to say that …?

4
Story-telling

Make two equal groups, A and B. Each group has a story to read or listen to – Group A's story is on page 79 and Group B's story is on page 80. Work together with a partner from your group. One student reads the story aloud while the other listens and takes notes.

With the others in your group, try to remember the story without looking at your book.

Now form a new pair, with one partner from Group A and the other from Group B. Tell your story to your new partner. Take notes and ask questions about the story you hear, to make sure you understand.

Now return to your original partner and compare notes on the story you have just heard. Finally, compare it with the one on page 79 or page 80.

5
It's your choice!

Your own vocabulary exercise

Choose interesting new words from this lesson or from your own reading. Write sentences, each sentence using one new word. Copy out the sentences with blanks where the new words are. Ask another student to guess the missing words.

Example

The blue light on top of the car was _____ on and off.
Answer: flashing

Pictures or mime

Choose one of the stories from this unit or make up your own story. Work with other students either to draw a series of pictures illustrating the story or to mime the story. When you are ready, show your mime/pictures to the rest of the class. Then ask the class to tell the story.

Your own grammar exercise

Read through the examples of the past perfect and past progressive that you listed in Exercise 2. Then make sentences using these verbs. Put the verbs in the infinitive form. Ask another student to put each verb into the right tense.

Examples

I (finish) the cooking before the guests arrived.
I had finished the cooking before the guests arrived.

I still (finish) the cooking when the guests arrived.
I was still finishing the cooking when the guests arrived.

Telling and writing a story

Work with a partner and make up a brief story like the ones in this unit. Tell your story to another pair and ask them to write the story.

6
Feedback

How well can you do the following activities in English? Rate yourself on this scale:

5 – Easily and enjoyably

4 – Easily

3 – Without too much difficulty

2 – With some difficulty

1 – With great difficulty

Activities	Score
Tell a simple story	
Listen to simple stories	
Read a simple story	
Take notes and write a story	
Encourage someone to continue a story	
Check that you have understood correctly	
Form and use the past perfect tense	
Form and use the past progressive tense	

In Self-study Workbook Unit 8 Grammar: past progressive, past perfect; intonation: expressing interest; classroom English: intonation; your own test: completing a paragraph; learning skills: listening.

REVIEW 2 Units 5-8

A
Progress check

Do the following activities to check your progress.

1 The person I most admire

Work with a partner. Take turns to speak for one minute about the person you most admire and why. The partner who is listening should time the speaker.

Score
Negotiate your score with your partner. Each of you can have up to 10 points for each of the following:

Content: interesting ideas, wide range of language

Accuracy: correct use of language

Fluency: speaking spontaneously and without hesitation

Add 5 bonus points for speaking for a whole minute without stopping.

If your score was 17 or less, look at Exercise 4 in Unit 6, and then try again.

Total score (out of 35): _____

2 Divorce

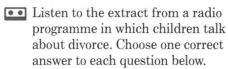 Listen to the extract from a radio programme in which children talk about divorce. Choose one correct answer to each question below.

Score
Check your answers on page 88. Give yourself 2 points for each correct answer.

How much did you understand when you listened?

80-100% (10 points)   20-39% (2 points)
60-79% (8 points)   0-19% (0 points)
40-59% (6 points)

Score (out of 20): _____

---

a) The parents think:

  1 If the marriage is bad, they should get divorced.

  2 If the marriage is bad, they should stay together for the children.

  3 They should stay together if the children want them to.

b) Louise feels:

  1 If the divorce is perfect, children can't complain.

  2 If your parents divorce when you're small, you grow up too quickly.

  3 If your parents live in a big house, they won't divorce.

c) Louise says:

  1 If she sees a family having fun, she wants to cry or scream.

  2 She is happy if she sees a film or reads a book about happy families.

  3 She is disappointed if she reads about a divorce.

d) Charlie says:

  1 It's better if he sees his father once or twice a week.

  2 It's better if he sees his parents as often as possible.

  3 It's better if he doesn't see his parents much.

e) Suzanne says:

  1 If she marries and has children, she'll try hard to make it work.

  2 If parents are like children, they shouldn't get divorced.

  3 She will get divorced if her children feel like she does.

3 Ask the expert

You are the expert who gives advice to readers of the magazine *Living*. Read this letter and write your reply, giving advice.

Score
Read your partner's writing and award a score as follows:

Up to 10 points each for:

Content: interesting ideas, good range of language, good advice

Accuracy: correct grammar, spelling, punctuation etc.

Style: appropriate language: not too formal, not too informal; range of appropriate expressions for giving advice etc.

Bonus points for length: add 5 points for every 50 words written, up to a maximum of 20 points for 200 words.

Score (out of 50): _____

Dear Expert,
My sister and brother-in-law have invited me and my boyfriend to go on holiday to Greece with them and their children. They are renting a villa with a private pool and we would only have to pay our airfare. My boyfriend wants us to go away on our own, but as he is short of money we couldn't afford anywhere as nice. He says if I loved him, I would want to be with him. I think he's being selfish in not understanding that I want a decent holiday. What should I do?
Meredith, London.

4 Tell a story

Work with a partner. Each of you should remember a story from Unit 8 and try to retell it to your partner. (Choose different stories.)

Score
Negotiate your scores. Give your partner up to 10 points for each of the following:

Content: Was it a good, interesting story? Did it have a good ending?

Fluency: Was the story told smoothly, without hesitations and repetitions?

Accuracy: Were the past tenses used correctly?

Bonus points for length: Score 5 points for talking for a minute or more.

Score (out of 35): _____

If your score is below 17, look back at Unit 8 and then try again.

5 Grammar check

Look at the following sentences. Some are correct and some have mistakes in them. Tick the sentences which are correct. Put a cross by the sentences which contain mistakes. Now try to correct the sentences with mistakes in.

a) This is what I'm going to say to you now.

b) She said him goodbye.

c) He told us about the misunderstanding.

d) My daughter started the school last week.

e) If you will be upset, tell someone.

f) If it is raining, take an umbrella.

g) If it will rain, you will need an umbrella.

h) He will be late if he misses that train.

i) If I were you, I wouldn't do that.

j) I would be sad if I wouldn't see you again.

k) They wouldn't like it if you don't come.

l) He was thinking about her when she had called.

m) They had just finished their dinner when the police arrived.

n) I couldn't open the door because I left the key in my other jacket.

o) The room was a mess; the children had left their toys everywhere.

p) Fred is walking down the road when suddenly he was attacked by some hooligans.

q) He said he was going to the doctor's.

r) He went to prison for life because he had murdered 16 people.

s) I feel sad that my parents had divorced.

t) Before she moved to Prague she had lived in Germany.

Score
Check your answers on page 88. Score 1 point for each correct tick or cross.

Score 2 points more for each corrected sentence.

Score (out of 30): _____

Now add up your total score:

150–170	**Brilliant!**
120–149	**Good.**
90–119	**Satisfactory.**
70–89	**Not bad, but don't forget to review the units regularly.**
0–69	**You definitely need to review Units 5–8 again.**

B
Checklist

Use this checklist to record how you feel about your progress.
Tick if you are satisfied with your progress. Put a cross if you are not satisfied.

I can	yes/no
describe people's characters, personalities and beliefs	
talk about my life and family	
talk about problems	
ask for and give advice	
tell a story or anecdote	
describe things that happened in the past	
understand the written texts in Units 1-8	
understand the recordings of spoken English in Units 1-8	

I know	yes/no
some useful expressions for asking for and giving advice	
more about my language learning needs	
more about my learning preferences	
more about how to use simple and first conditionals	
more about how to use second conditionals	
more about using the past tenses	
how to improve my listening	
how well I'm doing	

C
Personal plan

What problems do you have and how do you plan to help yourself?

Problems
_____
_____

Plans
_____
_____

9 That's not what I meant

Speaking
Talking about communication.

Grammar
Reported speech; question tags.

Vocabulary
Set phrases for talking about talking.

Listening
Active listening.

Learner training
Listening strategies; communication skills; practice in self-direction; self-assessment.

1
My favourite film

What is your favourite film? Work with a partner and tell each other the story of the film. Who are the main characters? What happens?

Activate your language
American English

The conversations from *Manhattan* contain these colloquial American expressions:

cut something off	= end something
a fling	= a short affair
screwed up	= disturbed
it's up your alley	= it suits you
you guys	= plural for men and women
wound up	= excited

2
Manhattan

Manhattan is a film by Woody Allen about friends living in New York. The friends are:

Ike (full name Isaac), who is divorced and has a girlfriend called Tracy

Mary, who is divorced

Yale who is married, and has been having an affair with Mary

a) Listen to this conversation between Ike and Yale as they play squash. They are discussing Mary. What does Yale say about himself and Mary? What does Yale suggest that Ike does? What is Ike's reaction?

b) What do you think happens next? Listen to the conversation between Ike and Mary and see if you were right.

c) The third conversation comes near the end of the film. Mary is trying to tell Ike something: what do you think this could be? Listen and check if you were right.

d) Look at the tapescripts for the three conversations.

Conversation A

Notice how Ike checks whether he has understood Yale by repeating what he says. Find two examples.

Conversation B

Mary says, 'Yeah, I know.' What is it that she knows?

Conversation C

What tells us that Mary wants to say something serious?

3
Reporting

Play 'Reported Speech Whispers' in a group of three. Student A whispers a statement in the present tense to Student B. The statement can be true or false. Student C cannot hear it. C asks B 'What did she/he say?' B tells C, using reported speech. C whispers a reply to B. A cannot hear it and asks 'What did she/he say?' B tells A using reported speech.

Example

A: I feel hungry.

C: What did she say?

B: She said she felt hungry.

C: I'm tired.

A: What did he say?

B: He said he was tired.

Swap roles so that everyone has a turn as B.

Activate your grammar
Reported speech

She said she found him attractive.
He said it was time to go.

In reported speech a number of changes are made:

1 Present tense verbs are changed into the past tense.
2 Pointer words can change: 'this' becomes 'that', 'now' becomes 'then', 'here' becomes 'there', and 'tomorrow' becomes 'the next day'.

Examples

Direct speech	Reported speech
'I find you attractive.'	She said she found him attractive.
'It's time to go.'	He said it was time to go.

See Grammar Review 13 on page 83.

4
Getting the message

Take turns to be Student A and Student B in this roleplay activity. Student A is expressing opinions on a subject and wishes to continue talking. Student B interrupts all the time to check that she/he has understood. Use the language from the 'Activate your language' section. Make up your own situations or use one of these:

A is telling the story of a film or book and saying why it is good or bad.

A is describing a recent sports event and commenting on it.

A has lots of ideas about how your town could be improved.

A has strong opinions about how people learn languages and about this English class.

Activate your language
Talking about talking

We use set phrases to indicate that we want to go on talking or to check understanding.

a) Showing you want to go on talking
Excuse me, but I'd just like to say that ...
There's something I want to say.
Just a moment, I haven't quite finished.
Hang on a second, there's something else ...
There's just one more thing ...

b) Ways of checking understanding
So what you're saying is that ...?
In other words ...
You feel that ...?
If I understand you correctly, ...
So you think that ...?
You're sure/confident that ...?
It seems to you that ...?
I'm not sure that I follow.
There's more to it, isn't there?
You're saying ..., aren't you?
You mean ..., don't you?
So the idea is ..., isn't it?

Activate your grammar
Question tags

A question tag at the end of a statement is an invitation to agree with it. The question is negative if the statement is positive:

You mean it's time to go, don't you?

The question is positive if the statement is negative:

You don't mean it's time to go, do you?

See Grammar Review no 14 on page 83.

5
Active listening

a) What is it that makes someone a good listener? Think of people you know. Who do you enjoy listening to? Who listens to you? How can you tell that someone is listening and paying attention to what you're saying?

b) Read this text about listening and consider the following questions:

1 What differences are there in ways of listening in different cultures?

2 How appropriate would it be in your culture to use the technique described here?

3 In what situations could you use this technique?

Learning tip

The next time you do pair work make sure that you are square to your partner and use the SOLER technique.

Active listening

The first step to being a good listener is illustrated by the story of Nan-in, a Japanese teacher of Buddhism.

One day a university professor came to visit Nan-in to learn about Buddhism. Nan-in served tea. He poured his visitor's cup full and then kept on pouring. Tea ran over on to the floor. The professor watched in horror and cried, "It is over-full. No more will go in!" "Like this cup," Nan-in said, "your mind is full of your own ideas and thoughts. You must empty it before you can start to learn."

The good listener concentrates on the speaker, not on his or her own thoughts.

In order to listen actively it is useful to think about the way you sit or stand. Good listeners use the SOLER technique.

S stands for SQUARE: facing the speaker shoulder to shoulder as in Figure 1. This is very important – think how many misunderstandings happen when people communicate side by side, in a car for example.

O stands for OPEN (Figure 2): sitting or standing with your arms down, or resting on your knees, not crossed (Figure 3). Try it, it's impossible to get angry if you're sitting with your hands resting on your knees!

L stands for LEANING: leaning slightly forward (Figure 4) is a sign of interest. Leaning back (Figure 5) shows lack of interest.

Fig. 1

Fig. 2

Fig. 3

Fig. 4

Fig. 5

E stands for EYE CONTACT. Look the person who is talking in the face — don't fix them with a rigid stare, but don't look away, or at the floor.

R stands for RELAXED and simply means being comfortable, not playing with your hands or chewing gum!

6
Listening to each other

a) Work in a group of three: a speaker, a listener and an observer.

Speaker

Tell a true or made-up story about something that happened to you. It may be something funny that happened to you or your family, the story of how you found your flat or car, how you met your partner, something that happened on holiday, an accident you were in, a journey you made, or a crime you saw happen.

Listener

Listen carefully, using SOLER and watching the speaker's whole person. Show that you are interested by nodding and smiling. Check that you have understood as you go along. Encourage the speaker by asking questions.

Observer

Watch both speaker and listener carefully. Note down any misunderstandings. Be ready to give feedback on how they spoke and listened.

b) After the speaker has told the story, the observer gives feedback to both speaker and listener on how well they did. Then change roles and repeat the activity.

c) After everyone has tried being speaker, listener and observer, have a short class discussion of the activity.

7
It's your choice!

Body language

Make a list of common gestures and facial expressions in your country. Next to each one, write what it means and when and where it can be used.

Making friends

Do a survey in your class of the ways in which people meet each other and become friends in your country. Use these headings as a guide:

Place

Activity

Time of day
and day of week

8
Feedback

Answer the following questions:

How did you feel about the activities in this unit?

Were some of the activities to do with English or with communication?

Can you try out some of the activities in your own language?

What do you think about the SOLER when you do pair work?

How did it feel having an observer when doing active listening?

Are there any activities here that you would like to do again?

The letter game

Play this game in a pair or small group. One student begins and says a word, any word. The next student has to say another word beginning with the last letter of the word, and so on.

Manhattan Part 2

Work with another student and continue the story of *Manhattan* from the end of the tapescript. Write out the dialogue and either act it out or record it on cassette for the other students to hear.

In Self-study Workbook Unit 9
Grammar: reporting verbs, question tags; reading comprehension; intonation: ending a telephone conversation; classroom English: reporting back; your test: making up words for a video.

10 Words and ideas

1

Born or became?

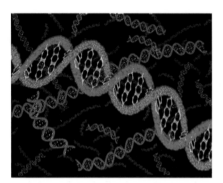

a) Read 'A gene for grammar?'. Can you complete the final sentence which begins: 'However, if true …'?

b) Do you believe that people are born as good language learners, or that they become good language learners through practice?

A gene for grammar?

Scientists and language researchers believe there may be a gene for grammar. Following 'discoveries' of genes said to be responsible for everything from intelligence to crime, this new finding must be treated with caution. However, if true …

2

Science and nature: genetic engineering

a) These extracts are from newspaper reports about ways in which scientists are changing nature. Match the following headlines with the extracts. You do not need to know every word in the headline: just check the headlines and extracts to see if the same words or phrases occur in both. Compare results with another student and say why each headline goes with a particular extract.

$2bn world-wide project leads torrent of breakthroughs

'Human' hearts bred in pigs for transplants

Frankenfood hits the menus

Baby to get first gene transplant
Operation aims to cure rare immune system deficiency

Race to design pigs that live on grass

1

Gene discovery has been accelerating at a tremendous speed since the launch of the Human Genome Project, an international $2 billion scheme to find all the 100,000 human genes. Many believe that the likelihood of getting cancer and heart disease is linked to genes. Some of the discoveries are unquestioned, some – usually those that involve social behaviour – are highly controversial.

2

Just when you thought it was safe to go back to the dinner table, 'Frankenfoods' are heading for the menu. Rainbow trout with human genes and tomatoes grown with genes from flounder fish are the latest product of food scientists. It is good news for producers – the trout grow bigger and more quickly, while the tomatoes have a lower freezing point, preventing them from becoming damaged.

3

In the laboratories of Newcastle University, scientists are trying to create a vegetarian pig, genetically engineered so it can eat grass. They are also claiming ownership of their pig, which joins a growing list of animal 'inventions' which scientists and commercial companies say cannot be copied without payment.

4

A baby girl will today make British medical history when doctors begin the first gene transplant designed to cure a deficiency which, untreated, could lead to her death. Carly Todd, aged eight months, from Lennoxtown, near Glasgow, has the same immune system deficiency which killed her 14-month-old brother four days before she was born.

5

Cambridge scientists have produced the world's first pigs containing human genetic material in an important step towards providing large supplies of hearts and other organs for transplant into humans. Two pigs with 'human' hearts have been born and are being kept at a secret location because of attacks by animal rights activists on scientists' homes.

Learning tip
Guessing

You can see that it is possible to match headlines with text without understanding all the words in the text. It is also possible to understand the general meaning of a word without knowing the exact meaning – most people know that genes are tiny things inside our cells which decide, for example, our hair colour or our height. A scientist will use a much more exact definition.

When we meet a new word we can ask for help or use a dictionary or guess. When we guess we can use our knowledge of other languages, our knowledge of English or the context. Take the first headline, for example:

$2bn world-wide project leads torrent of breakthroughs.

We can ask ourselves questions about words we do not know. For example:

'world-wide': what two words make up this word? Answer: 'world' and 'wide', so we can guess it means 'all over the world'.

'breakthrough': what two words make up this word? Answer: 'break' and 'through', so we can guess it is something to do with going through something, getting past something, going forward.

'torrent': does a '*torrent* of breakthroughs' mean a lot or a few? We can guess it means a lot – and this may be more helpful than using a dictionary, which will tell us that a torrent is a rush or flood of water!

Now try these:

'Frankenfood': does the word make you think of a monster? What was he called? So what kind of food is it?

'transplant': what other words do you know with 'trans' in them? 'Transport'? Is 'trans' to do with moving something or keeping it still? How about 'plant'? So what does 'transplant' mean?

Learning to guess well takes practice. It doesn't matter if you sometimes get things wrong. We all do. But guessing prepares you for the time when you don't have a dictionary or a teacher to consult.

b) Work with a partner and take one newspaper extract. Make up questions to help someone guess the meaning of some of the difficult words and try your questions out on other students.

c) Make a list of any new or difficult words in the five extracts. Work together with your partner to guess their meanings, checking your answers with a dictionary or the teacher.

d) Choose one of the following words/phrases from each extract. Write a short definition of each word/phrase as it is used in the extract.

Extract 1
accelerating, launch, unquestioned, controversial

Extract 2
menu, heading for, freezing point, damaged

Extract 3
laboratories, vegetarian, genetically, inventions

Extract 4
cure, untreated, immune system deficiency

Extract 5
step, organs, location, animal rights activists

Ask another student to match the definition and the word.

e) Work with a partner and make lists of the arguments for and against genetic engineering. Tell each other your opinions on:

changing genes to help cure disease

doing gene research on animals

changing genes to create different kinds of food

using parts of animals in human transplants

changing genes to change people's behaviour

doing gene research on people

Activate your language
Expressing opinions

1 **Stating your point of view**
  In my opinion, ...
  What I think/believe is that ...
  My view is that ...
  If you ask me, ...
  It's a question of ... -ing ...
  It's right/wrong to ...

2 **Stating your point of view strongly**
  The fact of the matter is that ...
  There's no doubt at all that ...
  ... can't possibly be right.
  ... is totally wrong.

3 **Giving a balanced view**
  It's a difficult question ...
  On the one hand ... and on the other hand ...
  There are no easy answers, but it seems to me that ...

Activate your grammar
Modal auxiliaries

There may be a gene for grammar.
It must be treated with caution.
Gene transplants might save lives.
You should not experiment on animals.
Who should decide what happens to the unborn child?

Possibility		Obligation	
might	may	should	must

➡ See Grammar Review 15 on page 84.

3
Animal rights

It's a magnificent breakthrough, professor!

a) Listen to the extract from a radio discussion programme called *Issues for Today* about experiments on animals. Which speaker do you agree with? Take a class vote on the issue.

b) Listen again, stopping where necessary, and complete these sentences:

Jeff Sachs

1 I believe that we experiment on animals because . . .

2 It's not that we think . . .

3 And it is dangerous to say . . .

4 Is it right to . . .

Dr Clark

1 Is Jeff arguing that . . .

2 Does Jeff want . . .

3 Is Jeff against . . .

4 If he isn't, why is it wrong . . .

c) Find a partner who has a different view from yours on experiments on animals. Tell each other what you think about the views expressed in the radio programme.

4
World problems

a) Work together as a whole class to make a list of at least five important problems in the world today (e.g. poverty, pollution).

b) Discuss the list with a partner and agree an order for the problems from 1, the world's most important problem, to 5, the least important problem. Write out your list in order from 1 to 5. Beside each problem write a reason for its position on the list. Compare your list with other students'.

c) Discuss with your partner possible solutions to each problem and write them on the list.

d) As a whole class, compare problems, reasons and solutions.

5
It's your choice!

Vocabulary

Choose one vocabulary area, for example medicine, and make a word network of the words linked to it.

Example

Word-building

The word 'unquestioned' occurs in this unit. Make lists of adjectives starting with the negative prefixes 'un-' and 'in-'.

Survey

Choose three of the problems from Exercise 4 and make a list of all the possible solutions for each problem. Then ask at least five students to grade the solutions for each problem on a scale of 1–5, where 5 = 'excellent' and 1 = 'poor'. Compare the results and draw a chart showing the results of the survey.

Imagine

Re-read Extract 4 in Exercise 2 and imagine you are one of Carly Todd's parents. Write a dialogue between yourself and someone who is against genetic engineering.

6
Feedback

How did this unit go for you? Fill in the chart with your comments.

Activity	How well?	Problems?	Solutions?
1			
2			
3			
4			
5			

In Self-study Workbook Unit 10
Grammar: modals and question formation; reading comprehension: question formation, for and against, questionnaire; pronunciation: words spelt differently but pronounced the same, word stress; classroom English: talking about pronunciation; your own test: stress marking.

11 Skills at work

Speaking
Discussing the use of English at work; taking part in meetings.

Grammar
Conjunctions and connectors; prepositions of time.

Vocabulary
Set phrases for use at meetings.

Listening
Listening to an interview for general understanding.

Learner training
Vocabulary learning strategies; practice in self-direction.

1
Jobs and skills

a) Make a list of five jobs that you find interesting.

b) Work with a partner. Student A mimes the job and Student B asks up to ten yes/no questions to help guess what the job is. Student A cannot speak, but can nod or shake her/his head to indicate yes or no.

c) Listen to the cassette. The speaker is describing the skills and personal qualities needed for a particular job. Note down as many of the skills and qualities as you can. Discuss them with your partner. What is the job? Is it doctor, police officer, journalist, nurse or actor?

d) Take five of the jobs which you mimed in (b). Make a list of the skills and personal qualities needed for each job. Show your lists to other students and ask them to guess what the jobs are.

Learning tip
Vocabulary

You may wish to learn some of the jobs or the words used to describe them in Exercise 1. The following techniques may be useful:

1 Write the each word on a small card. On one side write the word, on the other a sentence with the word missing. Put the cards in groups (e.g. jobs, sports, clothes, leisure activities) with 10 or 20 cards in each. Carry a different set of cards with you each day and look at them when you have a quiet moment.

2 Record the words in groups on a cassette and listen to them in your car or on a walkman.

3 Research shows that we learn words better if we have done something with them. Take the words for jobs and make two lists: jobs you would like and jobs you wouldn't like. Do the same with personal qualities: those you have and those you would like to have. Put the lists away and three days later try to write them out again.

4 Review new vocabulary the next day, one week later and one month later to keep it fresh. Look back now at Unit 1 Exercise 2 in the Self-study Workbook and see how many jobs you remember.

5 Use small (removable) sticky labels to label objects in the classroom and at home.

Experiment and see what works best for you.

2
English at work

a) Work with a partner and make lists of the uses of English in two of these jobs:

hotel receptionist	tour guide
secretary in an international company	sales representative for an international company

Try to be as detailed as possible: for example, not just 'Communicating with foreign customers' but 'Writing and understanding faxes and telexes in English'.

b) What work skills using English would you like to have?

c) For some of these work skills using English you will need specialised vocabulary (for example, the abbreviations used in faxes and telexes); for others (for example, business letter writing) you will need to get used to specialised forms of expression. However, one common problem in most work situations is communicating face-to-face or by telephone in English.

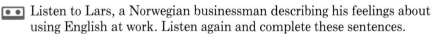 Listen to Lars, a Norwegian businessman describing his feelings about using English at work. Listen again and complete these sentences.

1 The last time he had to speak English at work was ...

2 He becomes very nervous whenever he ...

3 What makes him nervous is being ...

4 However, he doesn't get nervous when ...

5 He finds it easier to speak in meetings when ...

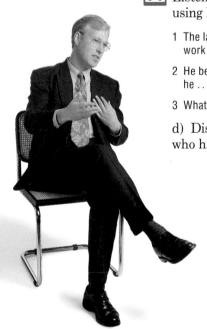

d) Discuss how you feel about using English. Find students in the class who have used English recently. Why? When? How did they feel?

3
Meetings in English

a) One of the most difficult things about meetings in a foreign language is that often by the time you have worked out what to say the discussion has gone on to another point. Read this text which gives some tips on how to interrupt and get your point across.

b) Work with a partner. How far do you agree with this advice? How does it compare with meetings in your own country?

HOW TO SUCCEED AT MEETINGS

Tip 1

Look at the person who is speaking and say 'I think that ...' while the person is still speaking. Stop and let the person carry on. Repeat this once or twice. Soon the other person will stop and let you say what you want to. Don't raise your voice, just repeat the start of your sentence.

Tip 2

Always sound as if you agree with the last speaker (even if you don't), and then say what you want. This will allow you to get your point across.

Examples

I agree with most of what you say. However, there is another way of looking at it ...

Yes, I see. Nevertheless, there is a lot to be said for looking at it differently.

Yes, I see what you mean. There's just one small point, however. Have you ever thought of ...?

That's quite clear. On the other hand, many people would say that ...

Tip 3

Present your viewpoint as if it was a summary of the meeting.

Examples

So what we're all really saying is that ...

In other words, we all feel that ...

So, although there is some disagreement, most of us agree that ...

Tip 4

Always pay compliments to the other speakers.

Examples

I think that what Hans said was very important.

We mustn't lose sight of what Lotta said.

Birgit put her finger on it when she said ...

4
Roleplay: equality at work

Do this in a group of about eight. Imagine that you all work for the same organisation. You are at a meeting to discuss this topic:

Equality at work: how can we improve the position of women in the organisation?

First decide what your organisation is. Is it a business, a factory, a shop, an office, a school? Is it in your country or in an English-speaking country? Choose a name for your organisation and write a one-sentence description of what it does.

Student A is the Chair of the meeting. The other students take roles B, C, D and E (one or two students for each role). Look at the role descriptions on pages 79–80 and read about your role.

Prepare for the meeting by making some notes. If two of you have the same role, discuss what you are going to say. Before starting the roleplay look through the text in Exercise 3 again.

The Chair starts the meeting by introducing those present.

At the end of the roleplay the Chairs report back to the rest of the class on the discussion and the conclusions reached, and the observers report on the language used and the way the participants behaved.

Activate your grammar
Conjunctions and connectors

However, there is another way of looking at it ...

Nevertheless, there is a lot to be said for ...

On the other hand, ...

Although there is some disagreement, ...

➡ See Grammar Review 16 on page 84.

5
Cultural survey: time

a) Work with another student to complete this survey. Complete the first column for your own country(ies), the second for Britain or the USA (guessing where you have to), and the third for another country.

Imagine you are going to these events. When do you arrive, before the time (B), exactly on time (T) or 15 minutes late (L)? Write the letters B, T or L in the columns.

b) Compare your survey results with other students'. What differences are there between the ideas of being on time in different countries? Are there differences between business and social appointments? What do the differences tell you about the different societies?

Event	Our country(ies)	UK/USA	Other
1 An appointment at an office			
2 Meeting a friend			
3 Dinner at someone's house			
4 A class at school/university			
5 The theatre			
6 A public meeting			
7 A date			
8 An office meeting of colleagues			
9 A party			

Activate your grammar
Prepositions of time

on time
in an hour
by midnight
for an hour
since seven
at eleven

➡ See Grammar Review 17 on page 84.

6
It's your choice!

Word chase

How many words can you write down in one minute for each of these topic areas?

Meetings	Jobs
Telephoning	Work clothes
Office equipment	Buying and selling
Computers	Office furniture

Compare your results with other students', and check the meanings of words they have which you don't.

English diary

Write down each occasion in the last week when you read, listened to, spoke or wrote English outside class. Use these headings:

When	What
Where	How I felt

Compare your diary with other students'. Have you thought of meeting out of class over coffee or a drink to use your English?

Non-stop talking

In a small group, write topics for discussion on small pieces of paper, fold them and put them in a pile. Then take turns to pick a topic from the pile and to speak on it for one minute in English. Continue until all the topics are used up.

In someone else's shoes

Put yourself in the place of each of the following people:

a single parent who cannot work because of the child

an office worker who is always late

a tourist guide who has difficulty explaining things in English

someone who has been in the same job for many years

Work with two or three other students. Take turns to imagine that you are one of these people. Tell the others what you feel and how you are thinking. Make up as many details as you can.

7
Feedback

How useful has this unit been for you? Grade the activities from 1 (useless) to 5 (very useful). Discuss your opinions with other students.

Activity	Grade (1–5)
1 Jobs and skills	
2 English at work	
3 Meetings in English	
4 Roleplay: equality at work	
5 Cultural survey: time	
6 It's your choice!	

In Self-study Workbook Unit 11
Grammar: conjunctions and connectors, prepositions of time; practical English: booking a hotel room; pronunciation: strong and weak forms of prepositions; classroom English: polite requests; your test: prepositions.

12

Clear communication

Speaking
Discussing gestures and effective communication.

Grammar
Present simple passive.

Vocabulary
Gestures and movements.

Reading
Reading a non-fiction text for general understanding.

Learner training
Self-assessment: reading; extensive reading; practice in self-direction; self-assessment.

1

The conference organisers

At a conference in a big hotel the letter of welcome to participants says, 'If you have any problem, however small, please ask the conference organisers for help'. Work in a group and take turns to be a conference participant. The others play the part of the organisers. The participant has something to ask or tell the organisers – but has lost her/his voice and must get the meaning across by mime.

Participant: Make up the message or ask the teacher for a message.

Examples of messages

Please wake me at four in the morning as I am going skiing.

There is a strange man asleep in room 101.

I would like to make a call to Russia at nine o'clock tonight.

Organisers: Ask questions and make suggestions to the participant in order to guess the message.

Listen to the example on the cassette.

2

Hand to face gestures

a) The text on page 55 looks at the way in which our body gives out messages when we speak. However, the paragraphs are in the wrong order. Match the pictures, the captions and the paragraphs to create the text. The pictures are in the right order.

Hearing, seeing or speaking a lie

Sucking

Boredom

Rubbing ear

Evaluation

Rubbing eye

Covering mouth

Stroking chin

Scratching neck

1

2

3

4

5

6

7

8

9

Hand to face gestures

a) When the listener begins to use his hand to support his head it is a signal that he is bored. Extreme boredom and lack of interest are shown when the head is fully supported by the hand. The ultimate boredom signal is given when the head is on the table and the person is snoring!

b) This is, in effect, an attempt by the listener to "hear no evil" – to cover the ear so as not to hear the words.

c) How can you tell when someone is lying? A clue is given by the three wise monkeys who hear, see and speak no evil. Human gestures are based on the monkeys' hand to face actions. In other words, when we hear, see or speak untruths or deceit we often attempt to cover our eyes or ears with our hands.

d) When you are next talking to a group of people, watch carefully. They will use evaluation gestures as you explain your ideas. But when you finish and ask for their opinions, the evaluation will cease. One hand will move to the chin and begin a chin-stroking gesture. This chin-stroking gesture is a signal that the listener is making a decision.

e) Evaluation is shown by a closed hand resting on the cheek, often with the forefinger pointing upwards. This can look similar to boredom – the difference is that here the hand is not supporting the head.

f) Sucking fingers, a pen, or glasses does not, however, indicate lying. It is a sign that the person is unhappy and wants help and reassurance.

g) Uncertainty or doubt is indicated by scratching the side of the neck. Our observation of this gesture reveals an interesting point: the person scratches about five times. It means "I'm not sure I agree," and is very noticeable when the words contradict it. For example, when the neck is scratched as the person says "I understand how you feel".

h) "See no evil," says the wise monkey. This gesture is used to avoid looking at the person who we are lying to. Men rub the eye and look at the floor. Women touch just below the eye and sometimes look at the ceiling.

i) This is one of the few adult gestures that is as obvious as a child's. The hand is used to cover the mouth in an unconscious attempt to stop the words coming out. Sometimes the mouth cover is disguised as a nose touch. If the person who is speaking uses this gesture, it indicates that he or she is telling a lie. If, however, the listener covers his/her mouth while you are speaking it indicates that he/she feels that you are lying.

Adapted from *Body Language* by Allan Pease

Activate your grammar

Present simple passive

A clue **is given** by the three monkeys.
The hand **is used** to cover the mouth.
Evaluation **is shown** by a closed hand.
The ultimate boredom signal **is given** when …

The passive is formed with the verb 'be' and the past participle. It is used to put information which we wish to emphasise at the start of the sentence.

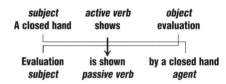

Note: The agent ('by …') can be left out.

➡ See Grammar Review 18 on page 84.

b) How do you feel about this text? How accurate is it about gestures in your country? Can you add any more meaningful gestures?

c) Work with another student. Sit facing each other and listen to the cassette. Obey the instructions, which use these verbs from the text:

cover	scratch	support
rest	stroke	touch
rub		

Then give each other instructions using the same verbs.

d) Read the text carefully, trying to memorise the information in it. Then work on your own and cover the text, leaving only the pictures. The pictures give you the structure of the text. Look at each picture and say quietly to yourself what the text said about it.

e) Work in a pair and use the pictures only to tell each other about hand to face gestures, according to the text. Demonstrate in front of the class, with one partner giving the talk and the other making the gestures.

3
Communication checklist

a) Below is a checklist of points to consider when speaking in a formal situation. Complete the checklist with verbs from this list:

give   present
look   speak
make   summarise
pause   treat
vary   work

Speaker's checklist

1 _____ out what to say.

2 _____ clearly.

3 _____ your voice.

4 _____ one idea at a time without complication.

5 _____ at the person from time to time.

6 _____ examples.

7 _____ to give time for questions.

8 _____ to help the person understand.

9 _____ the person with respect.

10 _____ sure the verbal message is the same as the non-verbal one.

b) Complete the listening checklist with words from this list:

bored   conversation   questions
clarification end   still
contact   feelings

Listener's checklist

1 Keep eye _____ with the speaker.

2 Face the person and be relaxed and open.

3 Don't interrupt.

4 Ask relevant _____.

5 Recognise the other person's _____.

6 Ask for _____ if you don't understand.

7 Don't appear critical, impatient or _____.

8 Sit or stand _____, don't fidget.

9 Don't 'take over' the _____.

10 Summarise at the _____.

c) Work in a group of three: a speaker, a listener and an observer. Take turns with each of the roles. The speaker talks about the topic for one minute. The listener listens carefully. The observer uses the checklists to watch and listen to the skills of the speaker and the listener and gives them feedback after the speaker has finished.

Suggested topics

How to cook a particular dish

What I'll do if I win $1,000,000

How to use a computer program

4
Self-assessment: reading

a) You can assess your own skills at reading and keep a record of your progress. First of all, think about these points:

Your reasons for reading

For pleasure? To understand the main idea? To understand every detail? In order to make or use something? Being sure of your reason for reading helps you use the right skills.

Your reading speed

Do you always read at the same speed or do you vary the speed according to the text type and your reasons for reading?

The kinds of text

Do you read a wide variety of texts? What kinds? Some people find it helpful to make a long list of different kinds of text and to practise on as many as possible.

b) Keep a record of your reading. Write down when you read in order to practise your English and also when you read English in a real-life situation. You may find that a table like this is helpful:

Date	Text	Reason for reading	Comments
3/11	Newspaper: sports news	To find out what happened at a football match.	I read slowly because I wanted to know exactly what hapened. But there were a lot of difficult words

c) You may also want to keep a record of what you do about reading problems, like this:

Problem	Action	Completed?
Difficult sports vocabulary	Make lists of words for different sports	Yes
Slow reading speed	Practise timing my reading	Yes

5
It's your choice!

Whispers

Work in a group of five or six. The first student writes down a two- or three-sentence message and then whispers the message to the second student, who whispers it to the third and so on, until the last student gets the message and writes it down. The first and last students then compare their messages.

Examples of messages

| an arrangement to meet someone | a description of an event, object or place | instructions |

Imagine

Work in a small group. If possible, play some quiet relaxing music. Close your eyes and imagine yourself using English successfully at work – either the job you have now or one you might get in the future. Live the scene in your imagination slowly. Then when the others are ready, tell them about your successful use of English.

Answer your own questions

Work in a small group. First prepare on your own. Imagine that you are an outside efficiency expert who is visiting the place where you work or study. Using your knowledge of the place, write a list of ten or more questions the expert can ask to find out how efficient your place of work or study is. When everyone is ready, give your questions to another member of the group who then asks you the questions. The others listen to the questions and answers, and give their opinions on how efficient your place of work or study is.

Reading programme

Work on your own. Borrow readers from your teacher or your class library if you have one. Look through the readers and find ten or more that look interesting. Make a plan to read one a day and keep a record of your progress, like this:

Date	Title	Done	Comment
3/11	Bristol Murder	Yes	Brilliant - very exciting

6
Feedback

Work with a partner and interview each other about your progress through this unit. Join another pair and find points that you agree on. Then join with another four to make a group of eight and note down the points that you *all* agree on. Each group of eight reports back to the teacher. Discuss how weak areas can be improved.

In Self-study Workbook Unit 12 Grammar: present simple passive; vocabulary: body movements; word-building: prefixes and suffixes; pronunciation: strong and weak forms of 'and' and 'but'; classroom English: correcting the teacher; your test: predicting.

REVIEW **3**

A
Progress check

Do the following activities to check your progress.

1 A misunderstanding?

 Listen to Carol describing what happened to her in Singapore. Then say if the following statements are true or false.

a) Carol said she'd had a lump on her left leg.

b) Carol said that she couldn't sleep because of the pain.

c) Carol explained that Singaporean doctors were very reassuring.

d) Carol described how the doctor cut off her leg.

e) The doctor told his assistant to take the lump to the laboratory for tests.

f) The doctor asked Carol to return in six days' time for the result.

g) Carol explained that she had missed her appointment at the hospital.

h) Carol described how calm she was when she asked for her results.

i) The assistant led Carol to believe it was cancer.

j) The assistant told Carol to speak to the doctor.

k) Carol described how scared she felt.

l) The doctor reassured Carol on the phone by telling her everything was fine.

m) Carol explained how she thought her situation was very serious because of what the doctors and the assistant had said earlier.

n) The doctor apologised on the phone for his assistant's misunderstanding.

o) The interviewer suggested there had been two misunderstandings, not one.

Score
Check your answers on page 89. Give yourself 2 points for each correct answer.

Total (out of 30): _____

2 What do you think?

Work with a partner. One of you is A and the other is B. First, A will listen to and time B speaking about one of the topics. When you are ready to start, A should choose a topic from the list and ask B to give her/his opinions about it for one minute without stopping. When B has finished, A should give a score. (This can be negotiated.) Then swap roles.

Topics

Frankenfood	Genetically engineered babies
Using parts of animals in human transplants	Doing gene research on animals

Score
Up to 10 points for content (was the speaker's opinion clear?)

Up to 10 points for accuracy

Up to 10 points for fluency

Plus 5 bonus points for talking for a whole minute without stopping!

Total (out of 35): _____

If you scored 17 or less, look back at Exercise 2 in Unit 10 and then try again.

3 Approach

Read the text below on the use of language at work, and fill in the gaps from the words in the list. More than one answer is possible for some gaps. Try to avoid repeating the same answer too many times or the text will sound unnatural.

first of all	however	lastly	such as
for instance	in addition	on the other hand	this
furthermore	in fact	so	

Approach

Many of us don't pay close enough attention to the effect our words are having on others. (a) _____ can be especially important if you are in a job where you have to deal with members of the public. (b) _____, what we call 'approach' is a combination of the language we choose to use, our behaviour and also our body language.

(c) _____, choosing the right language is vital for creating the right approach. The language we choose will depend on a number of factors, (d) _____ the situation we are in, who we are talking to and what their relationship is to us. (e) _____, what we want to do with the language (give directions, give information, ask for personal details, tell someone off, apologise etc.), the topic of the conversation and, (f) _____, how we feel at the time are all important influences in how we choose language. (g) _____, if we fail to make the right choice, we can sound rude and unpleasant. (h) _____, this can be bad for business.

(i) _____, sometimes we can give offence with our language without realising it. People become aggressive and we don't know why. One example of this is using language which may seem over-familiar. (j) _____, saying things like, 'Hello, love, what can I do for you?', or 'That'll be £2.30, ducks'. Calling people 'love' 'ducks' 'darling' etc. may seem to you to be friendly. You may even do it without noticing. These words are often used by men when addressing women they have never met before. Sometimes they are used by elderly women addressing younger people. They can be regarded by those on the receiving end as being patronising and belittling, (k) _____. Many women today are highly irritated by this kind of language. (l) _____, if you are in a job where you have female colleagues or are dealing with women members of the public, it is best to be aware that this kind of language can cause offence and steer clear of it.

Adapted from *You Can Cope! How to Deal with Aggression, Verbal Abuse and Offensive Behaviour at Work* by B. Sinclair

Score
Check your answers on page 89. Give yourself 2 points for each correct answer.

Total (out of 24): _____

4 Is it a lie?

Prepare for this activity individually and then work with a partner. First, think of a story to tell your partner about something which may or may not have happened to you. Your story must contain *five lies*. Make notes for ten minutes to prepare yourself. When you are ready, take turns to tell your stories. When you are listening to your partner's story, make a note of the lies you think you hear. Afterwards, check with the story-teller and negotiate scores, as follows:

Score
Speaker: Give your listening partner 2 points for each lie detected.

Listener: Give the speaker up to 10 points for sounding truthful and up to 10 points for speaking fluently with few hesitations.

Each partner should have a score as a listener and as a speaker.

Total (out of 30): _____

5 Grammar check

Tick the sentences which are correct. Put a cross by the sentences which contain mistakes and try to correct them.

a) You will come, won't you?

b) I'm on the list, too, aren't I?

c) Mimi didn't arrive on time, didn't she?

d) You like being called 'Ducks', wouldn't you?

e) Philip said he would read the book later.

f) The BBC told that divorce was increasing in the UK.

g) I must to go home right away.

h) The police informed them that the road might be clear by midnight.

i) Due to he was late, the dinner was spoiled.

j) Although he had many affairs, because they didn't get divorced.

k) I feel, however, that you have not worked hard enough on this.

l) On the other hand, he is a good actor, but on one hand he's not very good-looking, is he?

m) The director said he would see you on Monday on noon.

n) I'll be back in an hour.

o) My birthday's on 9th April.

p) What are you doing at the weekend?

q) The bell is rung every hour, on the hour.

r) The equipment are used all day long by the visitors to the gym.

s) The increase in the number of divorces is seen by most people as a problem.

t) What sort of food is ate in Thailand?

Score
Check your answers on page 89. Score 1 point for each correct tick or cross.

Score 2 points more for each corrected sentence.

Total (out of 30): _____

Now add up your total score:

130–149	Brilliant!
110–129	Good.
80–109	Satisfactory.
50–79	Not bad, but don't forget to review the units regularly.
0–49	You definitely need to review Units 9–12 again.

B
Checklist

Use this checklist to record how you feel about your progress. Tick if you are satisfied with your progress. Put a cross if you are not satisfied.

I can	yes/no
deal with misunderstandings	
use question tags correctly	
express my opinions	
take part in meetings	
agree and disagree politely	
give compliments	
use prepositions of time	
recognise and pronounce weak forms of prepositions	
use the simple present passive	

I know	yes/no
how to get my meaning across in a conversation	
some American colloquial expressions	
how to listen actively	
more about effective communication	
how to interrupt politely in meetings	
more about using connectors and conjunctions	
some different ways of learning vocabulary	
more about my learning preferences	
how well I'm doing	

C
Personal plan

What problems do you have and how do you plan to help yourself?

Problems
_____
_____

Plans
_____
_____

13 Stranger in a strange land

Speaking
Explaining the way
people behave in social
situations.

Grammar
Passive with modals;
past simple passive.

Vocabulary
Set phrases in social
situations.

Listening
Listening for detail.

Reading
Reading for general
understanding.

Writing
Writing a description.

Learner training
Self-assessment: writing;
practice in self-direction;
peer assessment of
writing.

1
Visualise!

a) Close your eyes and relax. You are on a visit to a foreign English-speaking country – maybe for business, maybe for pleasure, or a mixture of both. You are in your hotel room, with a lot of things to do today. What are they? Follow yourself through a day in which you are completely successful in your communication in English. Where do you go and how do you get there? Who do you speak to and how do they respond? Where do you have lunch and what do you order? What do you do afterwards …? Imagine the whole day and feel good about your successful use of English.

b) Work with another student and tell each other about your imaginary visit to a foreign country and how you feel about it.

2
A chance meeting on a plane

Using English for business successfully involves much more than a good knowledge of grammar and vocabulary. Sometimes things go wrong. Listen to what happens when two business executives meet on a plane.

a) Listen to the cassette and complete these sentences.

Where?
They are on a plane going from Tokyo to (1) _____.

Who?
Chu Hon-fai is from (2) _____. He is an (3) _____.

Andrew Richardson is from (4) _____. He is a (5) _____.

b) Now listen to the conversation and note down what the speakers say. Work in pairs and act out the conversation on the plane between the two businessmen.

c) Discuss how the two businessmen feel about the meeting. What does each think about the other? Then listen to the cassette and complete the notes below.

Mr Richardson
1 Pleased/not pleased about the meeting.

2 Happy/unhappy that he and Mr Chu _____
_____

3 Thinks that Mr Chu _____

4 Looks forward/does not look forward to meeting again.

Mr Chu
1 Pleased/not pleased about the meeting.

2 Comfortable/uncomfortable with Mr Richardson.

3 Thinks that Mr Richardson _____

4 Looks forward/does not look forward to meeting again.

d) Work with a partner. What went wrong between Mr Chu and Mr Richardson? Do you know of any similar examples of cultural differences? Tell each other or roleplay examples.

Name cards

Having a name card is almost as important to the Japanese as having a name. A man without a card is like a boat without a sail, or a fish without a tail. He is a person without identity. If you are a businessman it is essential that you get yourself name cards as soon as you arrive in Japan, or preferably before you leave home. Even if you are not in business, a name card is strongly recommended.

The name card to the Japanese is something that must be respected. Rolling someone's name card around your finger, or chewing a corner while you are talking to him, is ghastly behaviour. Name cards must be treated with respect as though they were living parts of the person whose name they carry.

The name card should be presented with two hands, and with a bow. Just before you present the card you introduce yourself with, for example, 'IBM *no* Ellen Lee'. *No* is the possessive word: IBM's Ellen Lee. The company name must be given first so it is best to use the Japanese form with the possessive word *no*. The natural English form, Ellen Lee of IBM, puts the personal name before the company's, which is not correct in Japan.

Your right hand should hold the card, with your left hand gently supporting your right hand. The card should be held so that the receiver can read it: upside-down to you. You bow as you present it, avoiding eye contact. And you say '*Dozo yoroshiku*' (Pleased to meet you) as you present the card.

When you receive another's card you take it with your right hand lightly supported by your left. You must bow again. You MUST look at it, even if you already know the person's name and company. It is a good idea to confirm the name by saying 'Nakayama-san *desu ne*?' (Mr or Mrs or Miss Nakayama, isn't it?). You'll get the pronunciation right that way, because the other person will repeat the name if you pronounce it wrongly.

The giving and the receiving of a card must not be done at the same time. The proper etiquette is to allow the other to present his/her card first, then present yours.

Adapted from *Culture Shock: Japan* by Rex Shelley

3
I am my name card

a) Do you have a business card? Is it common for business people in your country to exchange cards? When do people do this? What happens?

b) Read the text in order to find out about cards in Japan.

Work in a group on two paragraphs from the text. Check the meanings of any new words and make up five questions about your paragraphs to ask students from the other groups.

c) In Japan both giving and receiving a card are done in four stages. Tell each other what these stages are:

First ..., then ..., after that ..., and finally ...

Activate your grammar
Passive with modals

Name cards **must be treated** with respect ...
The name card **should be presented** with two hands ...
The card **should be held** so that ...
The giving and the receiving of a card **must not be done** ...

The passive used with modals is formed in the same way as the present simple passive. Where general rules are described, there is no agent.

subject	active verb	object	
You	must treat	name cards	with respect

Name cards	must be treated		with respect
subject	*passive verb*	*(no agent)*	

➡ See Grammar Review 19 on page 84.

4
Party time!

a) Complete these statements about party etiquette in Sweden. Then listen to Frank's description of a Swedish party to see if you were correct.

1 Guests should usually arrive _____

2 You should always bring _____

3 On arrival you have to _____

4 When drinking a toast you must _____

b) Read this summary of Frank's description. Listen again, underlining any parts of the summary which are incorrect.

Frank was invited to a party by his professor. He was told it was a summer party by the swimming pool, so he wore casual clothes. He arrived on time and brought the professor a bunch of flowers. Everyone at the party was dressed formally. Frank was introduced to the other guests by the professor. Before dinner, games were played on the grass and there was a great deal of conversation. During dinner a lot of wine was drunk. The winner of the games was announced: it was the professor. She was thrown into the swimming pool. After that everyone went home.

c) Rewrite the summary correcting the parts you have underlined.

Activate your grammar
Past simple passive

The winner of the games was announced. He was thrown into the swimming pool.

The form is the same as for the present simple passive, but with the verb 'be' in the past.

subject	*active verb*	*object*
The professor	**announced**	**the winner**

The winner	**was announced**	**(by the professor)**
subject	*passive verb*	*(agent)*

➤ See Grammar Review 20 on page 84.

5
Cultural quiz

What do you say in English to someone in these social situations? Discuss the situations and the best words to use.

Example

At Christmas   Happy Christmas!

Situations

1 Meeting someone for the first time

2 Before a meal

3 At New Year

4 On someone's birthday

5 Before drinking alcohol

6 On hearing someone has got a new job

7 On hearing someone has lost their job

8 Before an important interview

9 When someone is feeling ill

10 When someone has just sneezed

6
Self-assessment: writing

a) How do you feel about writing in English? In this course we concentrate on speaking and understanding, rather than writing. But everyone needs to write sometimes. Work with another student and make your own list of reasons for writing.

Examples

Filling out forms when I travel   Taking notes in class   Sending faxes

b) How many different kinds of writing in English do you need to do? List them under these two headings:

Writing to learn English   Using English to write

Grade yourself from 5 (excellent) to 1 (poor) for each kind of writing.

c) Look at the kinds of writing you have graded 1 or 2 (if there are any!). What are the problems here? Possible problem areas are:

Grammatical accuracy   Writing conventions

Accurate vocabulary   Style

d) Write a brief description of behaviour in a social situation in your country, explaining it to a foreign visitor. Keep this piece of writing with you – you will need it for the feedback activity in Exercise 8.

Learning tip
Grammatical accuracy

The problem with writing is that you have to be accurate. When you're speaking people can see your face (unless you're on the phone) and get a lot of your message from your body language. Also when speaking there's no chance to go back and check something for mistakes: you are always going forward. Speech is also a two-way process – you can always ask someone to repeat or explain. When you write, people expect you to be correct for these very reasons: they can't check something with you personally, but they can look back carefully over what you've written so any mistakes show up. This means that you have to do the same with your own writing: be very clear about what you want to say (plan carefully) and check and re-check what you've written.

Accurate vocabulary

When you're speaking you can always explain what a word means or use a different word if you see that the listener doesn't understand you. In writing you don't get this chance to clear up misunderstandings, so you have to be clear and accurate in what you say. There's little point in writing 'a kind of big flat thing we sleep on' when you mean 'bed'.

Writing conventions

This simply means spelling, punctuation and layout. These are things which all learners of English writing have to master, whether English is their first, second or tenth language!

Style

Writing is usually more formal than speaking (unless you're writing on the walls or speaking in court!) and it is important that the kind of language used is appropriate. In many ways stylistic mistakes are the most important.

Some suggestions

Dictation is a great confidence builder. Do regular self-dictations where you record a passage and then write it out; or get another student to dictate to you.

Collect models of the writing you need to do: letters, faxes, forms etc. Copy and imitate them.

For each different kind of text write out useful expressions and learn them: for example, ways of beginning a letter.

Look back through writing you have done and find the words you have spelt wrongly. Make lists of the correct spellings.

Write several drafts of a piece of a written work, checking them yourself and asking others to check for you.

Use a word-processor if you can, so that it is easy to make lots of changes and have an attractive end-product.

7
It's your choice!

Roleplay

Work with a partner. One student is a foreign visitor to your country, the other is looking after the visitor. The visitor asks for explanations of local behaviour (for example, meals, shopping, parties, transport, holidays).

References

A reference is a letter to an employer recommending a person for a job. Work with other students to agree on a job. Then work with a partner to write a reference for another student in the class for the job. Do not mention the student's name (use X) but mention lots of things about her/him. Begin:

I am very pleased to write a reference for X for employment as (name of job).

As a group, try to guess who each reference is about.

Word-building

Prefixes come at the start of words and change the meaning (for example, 'mis-' changes 'understand' to 'misunderstand') and suffixes have the same role at the end of words (for example, '-less' changes 'help' to 'helpless'). Look back through earlier units in this book, other books in English and, if necessary, a dictionary and try to find as many prefixes and suffixes as possible.

8
Feedback: assessing each other's writing

Work in a small group. Exchange copies of the writing you did in Exercise 6(d). As you read each piece of writing, underline in pencil anything you don't understand or are not sure about. Then ask the writer to explain what is underlined and, if necessary, to make changes. When everyone in the group has read all the pieces of writing and rewritten their own, look at them again. Discuss which piece of writing best describes how to behave for a foreign visitor.

National stereotypes

Work alone or with a partner to list national stereotypes – ideas or images of nationalities around the world. For example, the English are often seen like this: formally dressed with a hat and umbrella and thought to be unable to show their feelings. Beside each stereotype on your list give an example, if you can, and say if you agree with it or not, giving reasons.

Discuss the stereotypes with other students. How true are they? Why do people classify other people?

In Self-study Workbook Unit 13
Grammar: passive infinitive with modals, past simple passive; listening comprehension; vocabulary: shape and position; pronunciation: word stress; classroom English: correction symbols; your test: punctuation and layout.

14 It's in the news!

Speaking
Talking about events in the news.

Grammar
Present perfect passive; past perfect passive.

Vocabulary
The language of news reports and newspaper headlines.

Listening
Listening to news broadcasts for gist and detail.

Reading
Reading headlines and news reports for gist and detail.

Writing
Shortening and summarising texts.

Learner training
Listening strategies; practice in self-direction; self-assessment.

1

The news today

a) What is in the news today? Work in a pair or small group to make a list of the main topics of the news today. Think about the TV or radio news and newspapers, in your own language or in English.

b) For each main topic write down the following information:

Where? (in which town or country?)

Who? (who is the news about?)

What (what has happened?)

When? (when did it happen?)

Examples

1 Where? Italy

   Who? Thousands of people

   What? Have been made homeless by floods

   When? In the last two days

2 Where? Sydney, Australia

   Who? Three American hostages

   What? Have been freed by Australian police

   When? After a gun fight with kidnappers

3 Where? New York

   Who? The pilots of a USAir plane

   What? Made an emergency landing because they didn't have enough fuel

   When? Yesterday

c) Compare your information summaries and write headlines to report the news.

Examples

1 **Thousands homeless**

2 Hostages freed

3 **USAIR EMERGENCY**

Activate your grammar
Present perfect passive

Thousands of people have been made homeless by floods.
Three American hostages have been freed by Australian police.

The use of the passive here focuses attention on the people to whom something has happened.

subject	active verb	object	
Floods	have made	thousands of people	homeless

Thousands of people	have been made	homeless	by floods
subject	passive verb		agent

The present perfect (active or passive) is often used in the first sentence of a news report to show that the event is very recent - it emphasises the link between the past and the present.

➡ See Grammar Review 21 on page 85.

2
Not the news

a) Listen to this news report of events which are definitely *not* from today's news. Listen once for general understanding. Then listen again, stopping after each event, and complete the table.

b) Make up three imaginary news stories and tell them to another student.

Event	a) Where?	b) Who?	c) What?	d) When?
1				
2				
3				
4				

3
Making headlines

a) Here are the beginnings and endings of some real newspaper headlines. Make new headlines by joining up as many beginnings and endings as possible.

Beginnings	Endings
Two injured	higher marks
Girls get	at White House
Movie star	injures foot
£1m plan	dismissed
Drug offence plot	as train crashes
Queen	found dead
Hope	in US plane crash
Three hostages	to save lives
68 dead	for baby smugglers
Shots fired	rescued

b) Make up news stories to go with the headlines, saying as much as possible about what happened. Then choose one headline and write a paragraph to go with it. Save your paragraph to use in Exercise 4(c).

4
Sub-editors

The job of a sub-editor on a newspaper is to make up the headlines and to make sure that the news stories are the right length to fit the page. They often have to cut stories (reduce the number of words). For example, this story needs to be shortened to less than 45 words:

Plague-free

INDIA: Eight weeks after two outbreaks of bubonic plague spread fear around the world, India has declared it is plague-free.

Airline routes to many parts of the world were cut, thousands fled their homes, and 57 died during the scare. The news has been reported to the World Health Organisation which will issue a statement in due course.

(61 words)

So a sub-editor might shorten it to this:

Plague-free

INDIA: Eight weeks after two outbreaks of bubonic plague spread fear around the world, India has declared it is plague-free.

Thousands fled their homes and 57 died during the scare. The news has been reported to the World Health Organisation.

(43 words)

a) Choose one of these texts, write a headline for it, and work with another student to cut the length to 100 words or less.

1 At least 50 people have been killed and thousands made homeless during the worst rainstorms to hit north-west Italy in 80 years. The death toll from floods and landslides could rise to 100, it was feared today.

Rescuers have been searching for twelve people missing in the countryside around the city of Turin. Rescuers had little hope of finding them alive, as no survivors had been found by evening.

Italian TV forecast that the death toll could rise as high as 100 when floodwaters went down. 'The official figure is 35 dead and about a dozen missing,' said Ombretta Fumagilli Carulli, Under-Secretary for Civil Protection. 'But we can say with certainty that the numbers of victims will rise.'

Italian officials said the rainstorms on the north-west coast were among the worst this century. Rain had been falling steadily for several days and yesterday half a metre of rain fell in many areas in just two hours.

(156 words)

Adapted from Cambridge Evening News

2 A bridge in the centre of Seoul collapsed yesterday, killing 32 people as cars and a bus fell into the river. The mayor of Seoul resigned after at least 32 people were killed and 17 injured when a bridge in the centre of the capital collapsed.

Commuters watched in horror as the central part of the four-lane Songsu bridge plunged into the Han river, taking with it cars, vans and a full bus.

'I don't want to think of this nightmare again. How could a bridge which millions of citizens use every day collapse so easily?' said a school-teacher, Kim Min-ja. Mrs Kim had been saved by rescue boats after the car in which she was travelling fell off the bridge into the dark waters below. She managed to get out of the car and swim to safety.

Poor construction work has been blamed for several South Korean building disasters. Only recently questions have been asked in parliament about the safety of the 17 bridges which cross the Han in Seoul. The construction minister, Kim Woo-suk, said there was no cause for concern.

(183 words)

Adapted from The Guardian

b) Compare your version of the story with other people's.

c) Work with another student and exchange the paragraphs you wrote in Exercise 3(b). Sub-edit your partner's paragraph to shorten it and, if necessary, change the headline.

Activate your grammar
Past perfect passive

No survivors had been found by rescuers.
Mrs Kim had been saved by rescue boats.

The passive is also used here to focus attention on the more important people involved.

subject	active verb	object
Rescuers	had not found	any survivors

No survivors	had been found	by rescuers
subject	passive verb	agent

➡ **See Grammar Review 22 on page 85.**

5
News 2010

a) You are going to listen to a TV news broadcast from the year 2010. The topics are listed below. Discuss each topic with another student and predict what the news will be. Write notes in the 'Prediction' column of the chart.

b) Then listen and take notes in the 'Broadcast' column. Stop after each news item and see if it changes your predictions for the following ones. Afterwards compare your predictions with the broadcast.

Topic	Prediction	Broadcast
1 The Queen		
2 The weather		
3 Switzerland		
4 Finance		

6
It's your choice!

This is the news

Work in a pair or small group. Listen to a recording of the news in English and write down exactly what is said, stopping and starting as often as you need to. Then either make up questions about the news or copy out part of it with some words missing. When you are ready, invite other students to listen and answer the questions, or fill in the words.

The world news

Work in a small group and prepare a short radio news broadcast about the world news today. You may wish to include 'real' news about the other students in the class. Record your news broadcast on a cassette and play it to the other students.

Newspaper questions

Work in a pair or small group. Read quickly through an English language newspaper and write a list of six questions about the articles in it. Put your questions with the newspaper. When everyone is ready, the papers are passed around and you answer the questions made up by the other students.

Cultural comparisons

For this you need at least one copy of a newspaper in English and one in your own language. Alone or with a partner, compare the newspapers and see what differences you can find. What do the differences tell us about differences between countries?

7
Feedback

It is important to be realistic about how much we can expect to understand from news broadcasts and newspapers in a foreign language. Being able to understand the main points, or just what the topic is, is often enough. That will help us find any items which particularly interest us and which we can read or listen to more carefully.

How well did you understand the news in this unit?

Learning tip
Listening strategies

Look back through the listening tasks in Units 1-13 and note down the advice given about listening and the different ways in which listening is approached. Make a list for yourself of the kinds of listening texts you want to work on and the strategies you will use with the texts.

Exercise	Understood everything	Understood enough	Understood a little	Understood nothing
2 (listening)				
4(a) (reading)				
5 (listening)				

What will you do to improve your understanding of the news?

In Self-study Workbook Unit 14
Grammar: present perfect passive, past perfect passive; listening: the sub-editor's job; vocabulary: the weather; pronunciation: countries and nationalities; classroom English: definitions; your test: matching headlines and articles.

15 Progress?

Speaking
Evaluating past predictions and discussing future inventions.

Grammar
Future passive; future perfect passive.

Vocabulary
Inventions and discoveries.

Listening
Listening to short descriptions for accuracy.

Writing
Producing a questionnaire; writing a letter.

Learner training
Group and self-evaluation; practice in self-direction; self-assessment, activity evaluation.

1

Predicting the future

a) What was life like about a hundred years ago? How many of these things existed?

television	aeroplane	washing machines
telephone	vacuum cleaner	radio
motor car	railways	

b) In 1893 a Chicago newspaper asked 74 of America's best minds to predict life at the end of the twentieth century. One writer saw the future of air travel like this:

'Considerable travelling will be done in the air. The balloons will be guided from city to city by a wire strung thirty metres above the ground, so as to let the balloon pass over trees and houses.'
(David Swing, preacher)

Another looked forward to more peaceful times:

'It will be possible for women to walk from house to house, in city or country, in safety. Girls will be able to go to church or to school, or even take a harmless walk in the field or woods, without danger of being attacked and murdered.'
(Elizabeth Allen, poet)

Imagine it is 1893. Work in pairs and make predictions about life at the end of the twentieth century. Think about houses and transport, communications, work, leisure, world and national politics. Make a list of your predictions.

Activate your grammar
Future passive

Considerable travelling will be done in the air.
The balloons will be guided from city to city by a wire.

The future passive is formed in the same way as other passives.

subject	active verb	object	
A wire	will guide	balloons	from city to city

Balloons	will be guided	by a wire	from city to city
subject	*passive verb*	*agent*	

➡ See Grammar Review 23 on page 85.

c) Join up with another pair and discuss your predictions. Compare what you predicted with what has actually happened.

Examples
'There will be enough food for everyone.'
We said that there would be enough food for everyone, but there are still terrible famines in some parts of the world.

'People will have electric cars.'
We predicted that people would have electric cars, but most cars still use petrol or diesel.

Activate your language
Reporting predictions

We thought/said/believed/predicted that ... would ...

d) Now imagine it is 1945. Work in pairs and make and compare predictions about life today on the following topics and others of your choice.

Communism   Disease

Space travel   Computers

e) Now predict life in a hundred years' time. Work in a pair, then in a group, to make a list of predictions that everyone in the class agrees with.

Examples

Disease will have been wiped out.

People will be living on the Moon.

Africa will be the richest continent and Europe the poorest.

There will have been a world war.

Activate your grammar
Future perfect passive

In a hundred years' time disease will have been wiped out.

The future perfect tense expresses the past in the future.

Disease	Disease wiped out	No disease
Now		**100 years later**

There is disease now – but it is predicted that in 100 years' time there will be no disease. People will be able to look back and say 'Disease has been wiped out'. So *now* we can predict: 'In a hundred years disease *will have been* wiped out'.

➡ **See Grammar Review 24 on page 85.**

2
Inventions and inventors

a) What do you think are the ten most important discoveries or inventions of the twentieth century? Work with a partner and make a list, with reasons.

Example
We think nuclear energy was one of the most important discoveries because it can destroy the world.

b) Inventors are not always sure of the uses to which their inventions can be put. Read the following text.

CDs have taken over from records, which developed from a machine called a phonograph. However, the inventors of the phonograph never thought it would be used for music! The inventor of the phonograph was Thomas Edison in 1877 and he wanted to use it 'to make Dolls speak, sing and cry and make various sounds'. He had no success. Then Alexander Graham Bell, the inventor of the telephone, tried. He thought the phonograph could be used as a talking fire alarm! Edison tried again and thought the phonograph could be used as a business dictation machine. Ten years later a music recording by Caruso sold a million copies!

Work with a partner and think of other possible uses for everyday household objects and machines like the ones in the picture. See which pair can think of the strangest use for the most ordinary object.

3
Spot the fake!

Inventions are often named after the inventor. Listen to these descriptions of the lives of the inventors of denim, the hoover, ketchup, the kiosk, the sandwich and the walkman. Which are true and which are fake?

4
Group inventions

a) Work with a partner to invent something useful. It can be any size, shape or cost. It can be of practical use (e.g. a car which folds up into a suitcase) or for fun (e.g. skis with motors to help you go uphill). Discuss various possibilities and choose one.

b) Use a large piece of paper to make a detailed drawing of your invention. The drawing must be careful and accurate. Give the invention a name and, if necessary, write operating instructions, but do not write what its purpose is.

c) Display your drawing and look at the other drawings. Try and guess the purpose of the other inventions.

5
Group self-evaluation

a) Look back at your aims for learning English which you discussed in Unit 2. How far do you feel that you have achieved those aims?

b) Look back at Units 1–14. How easy/difficult do they seem now? If possible, listen again to extracts from the cassette for these units.

c) Work with another student or in a small group and write a letter to an imaginary new student starting work with this book tomorrow. What information and advice would you give to the new student? Write about the units, the cassette, the Self-study Workbook, about what to do in class and how to work outside class. Keep this letter – you will need it for Unit 16.

d) Work alone and then with the whole class to make up a questionnaire about the course. The aim of the questionnaire is to help the teacher plan a future course and to know which activities and techniques were most successful. Each student suggests two questions and these are written on the board. Then the class works together to cut out questions about the same topics. Copy out the questions, do the questionnaire for yourself and bring the answers to the next lesson.

6
It's your choice!

Cultural comparisons

Take three countries in different continents of the world. Imagine what inhabitants of these countries would predict life to be like in 50 years' time. How are the predictions different? How are they different from your own predictions?

Unlinked words

We can make all kinds of links between words. For example:

pen → paper → present → Christmas → snow → ski → TV → cartoon → mouse → cat

The aim here is the opposite: to think of words with no links between them at all. Work in a group of three. Student A says a word and Student B has to say a word that has no possible link with the first word. Then A replies with a word that has no connection with B's word – and so on. Student C listens to make sure that there is no connection between the words.

New words

Work with a partner to invent new 'English' words. For each word you invent, write a definition and give an example using it in a sentence. Then separate the words and definitions and ask another pair to match them. If you wish, you can use a dictionary to add one real English word and definition to the invented ones.

Describe and draw

Work with a partner. Student A makes a simple drawing using geometrical shapes, or draws the same thing twice with some differences. Student A then describes the drawings (without showing them) to Student B who tries to copy them. Then compare the copy and the original.

7
Feedback

a) Feedback is important for both students and teachers. How can you give feedback to your teacher? How can you help her/him evaluate her/his performance? Discuss in a pair or small group and consider these issues:

How aware was the teacher of learning differences within the group?

What did the teacher do to help keep a good group feeling?

How far did the teacher keep in touch with the feelings of the whole class, and with each individual within it?

b) Prepare feedback for the teacher under these headings:

Positive things I'll remember about this class

Some things that did not work for me as an individual

Some things I have learnt from you and from the others

For Unit 16

Bring to class the letter you wrote in Exercise 5(c) and the questionnaire which was made by the class in Exercise 5(d).

In Self-study Workbook Unit 15
Grammar: future passive, future perfect passive, reported statements; reading: punctuation and capital letters; vocabulary: phrasal verbs with 'over' and 'out'; pronunciation: minimal pairs; your test: revision.

Speaking
Discussing past learning
experiences and planning
the future.

Grammar
Future progressive.

Vocabulary
Feelings.

Reading
Reading letters.

Learner training
Consideration of the
language learning
process; experiment
in creating a 'new'
language; practice in
self-direction; self-
assessment.

1
The first time

a) Think back to the first time the class met for a lesson. Where were you sitting? Who were you sitting with? What were you wearing? Can you remember any sounds or smells? Work with another student and try to remember as many details as possible.

b) How were you feeling at this first lesson? What did you expect and hope for? What were you afraid of?

c) And how do you feel now? How about your hopes and fears at the start of the course? Have they come true? Work in a pair, then with the whole class.

Examples
I thought it would be difficult for me at the beginning and it was. But things soon became easier.

I was afraid of making a fool of myself at the start. But after a little while I stopped worrying.

Activate your language

I was feeling rather/a bit + adjective
I hoped that I/it would be + adjective
I expected it to be + adjective
I was afraid it might be very/too + adjective
I was afraid of + '-ing'

afraid apprehensive frightened shy timid worried

exciting stimulating effective demanding time-consuming

appearing silly/foolish/slow

not knowing what to say/do

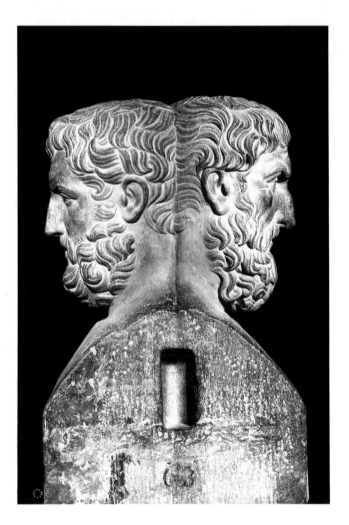

2
Letters to the next group

a) Exchange the letters you wrote in pairs in Unit 15, Exercise 5(c). Read as many letters as you can. Note down things you agree with and things you disagree with.

b) Work in a pair or small group and discuss your reactions to the letters.

3
It's been good!

a) 'I'll always remember when ...

Work with a partner and share your memories about amusing or interesting events during the course by completing this sentence in as many ways as possible. Write out the most amusing memories and exchange them with other pairs.

b) 'What I'll remember about you is ...'

Take one sheet of paper for each student with that person's name at the top. Pass the papers around the class and write on each paper except the one with your own name on. Write something positive which you will always remember about the person: it may be something that happened, something they wore or something they said.

Examples

The day when you brought your dog to the class

Your big red sweater

4
What I've learnt about language learning

a) Work with a partner and discuss what the course has helped you discover about how you learn languages.

b) Compare with other pairs and make a whole class list of the things you've learned. Keep the list for the next exercise.

5
Novolingua

a) Work in one of four groups, A, B, C and D. You are going to make up and teach each other a new language! Don't worry – not the whole language, just four sentences!

First, work together in your group to create your language. It can be completely new, or it can be similar to or based on a language you know. The important thing is that no one in the other groups must know it. Make up your four sentences – they can be about the same topic or different topics. Learn the sentences by heart (so it's a good idea to keep them short) and each write them out carefully on a piece of paper. Test each other on your 'knowledge' of the new language.

b) Now form a group of four, containing one student from A, one from B, one from C and one from D. Take turns to teach each other the four sentences in your 'language'. You can use movement or gesture to explain but you must not use English or your own language *except* to answer questions in English with a 'yes' or 'no'. You must not translate the sentences.

c) When you have finished, discuss the experience with other members of your group. Have you found out anything about teaching and learning languages? Look at the list you made in Exercise 4(b). Is there anything you want to change or add?

d) Share your conclusions with the whole class.

6

In five years' time

a) Where will you be in five years' time? What will have happened by then? What will you be doing? Where will you be living? Where will you be working, or what will you be studying?

Work on your own and think about yourself in five years' time, and then about the other students in the class. What will they be doing?

b) Form a pair. Tell your partner what you think she/he will be doing in five years and see if she/he agrees. Listen to your partner's prediction for you and correct it if necessary.

Examples

In five years' time you'll have graduated from university.

I expect you'll be working abroad. I hope it'll be somewhere nice.

c) Work with a partner and plan a party where all the class can meet again in five years' time. Plan the party details and predict who will come with who and what they will be wearing.

Activate your grammar
Future progressive

What will you be doing?
Where will you be working?
I expect I'll be working abroad.

The future progressive is formed with 'will be' + verb + 'ing'. It is used to refer to events which will be routine in the future ('I'll be working abroad') and to events in the future which are already planned ('I'll be leaving at six o'clock').

➡ See Grammar Review 25 on page 85.

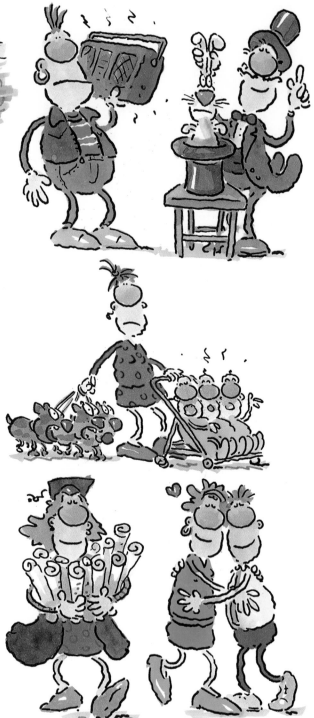

7

Your future learning

a) With a partner, plan your English language learning and practice aims over the next five years, a year at a time. Help each other with suggestions for ways of working on your own or with others.

b) If possible, work with someone who you will keep in contact with after the course. Write a short plan of your English practice over the next year beginning 'I promise that I will …' and give it to the other student.

8
It's your choice!

Now and then

Choose an activity from Units 1–10 and do it again. With other students discuss your feelings and how well you did.

Map of the book

Go carefully through the Map of the Coursebook on pages 4–5, noting areas where you need to do more work and areas where you feel you are on top of things. Remember to judge yourself now against how you were at the start of the course – not against some imaginary perfect English speaker!

Praise praise praise

Work in a group and give each other positive feedback on the progress made over the course. Give as many examples as you can.

My report

Imagine that you are the teacher. Write a report by the teacher on you and your progress in English during this course. Show the report to your teacher.

9
Feedback

a) Work in a small group to analyse the answers to the questionnaires which you created in Unit 15, Exercise 5(d). See how many opinions are shared and how many are different. If you are not sure about the meaning of a question or answer, ask the person who wrote it.

b) As a whole class, compare the results from the different groups, and give the individual questionnaires to the teacher.

10
Farewell

Sit in a circle of the whole class. If possible, listen to some quiet music. Then slowly, one after the other, tell each other what you will be doing and what you will be thinking at exactly this time next week.

In Self-study Workbook Unit 16
Grammar: future progressive; future perfect; your future English language learning; listening: the Carioca goodbye, how to say goodbye; pronunciation: friendly goodbyes; classroom English: the language of reports; your test: remembering the book.

REVIEW 4

A
Progress check

Do the following activities to check your progress.

1 Dictation: etiquette in Fiji

🔲 Listen to the first reading of the text, which is at normal speed.

🔲 Now listen to the second reading and write down what you hear. The reader will pause for you to do this and then repeat each phrase.

🔲 Finally, listen to the third reading of the text and check what you have written.

Here are three Fijian expressions from the text. Can you guess what they refer to?

kava root   yaqona   bure

Score
Check your dictation on page 89. Start with 50 points. Take off 1 point for every spelling and punctuation mistake. Give yourself an extra 5 points for guessing correctly what each of the Fijian expressions above refers to.

Total (out of 65): _____

2 In the news

Read the following extract from a newspaper once only. Then, without looking at the text, make notes under the headings below.

a) Where?   b) Who?   c) What?   d) When?

e) Why?   f) Opinions expressed

Two-tests plan to cut car death crash toll

Learner motorists will face an extra driving test before they are allowed behind the wheel alone. Young drivers, who account for a far greater number of road deaths and accidents than their numbers warrant, are the main target in the biggest shake-up of the driving exam since it began 60 years ago. From July next year they will have to pass a 30-question written exam in special classrooms before they are allowed to take the driving test proper. The move will be announced on Tuesday by the Junior Transport Minister, Steven Norris. It is the brain-child of Transport Secretary Dr. Brian Mawhinney, who is determined to cut the annual death toll on UK roads from the current 3,800.

Figures given to him show that most of the 500,000 people who take the current driving test each year are aged between 17 and 25. And this is the age group which makes up 25 per cent of all road deaths and 20 per cent of all traffic accidents. In future, instead of answering a few verbal questions put by examiners, L-drivers will answer multiple choice questions covering a range of safety concerns, driver attitudes and environmental issues, as well as many old favourites from the Highway Code, such as braking distances and sign identification.

The only disappointment expressed by the Automobile Association was that the government test had not gone further. Andrew Howard, head of road safety for the AA, said that research showed that youngsters took twice as long to anticipate hazards than older, experienced drivers. "Young drivers have this blind belief that the other car is always going to stop. Of course, it often doesn't." He wants an interactive CD-Rom video display system developed to help young drivers improve their hazard awareness. "The trouble with a paper-based system is we could be stuck with it for ever."

Adapted from *The Mail on Sunday*

Score
Check your answers on page 90. Give yourself up to 5 points for each answer – 0 points for no answer, 5 points for a very full answer.

How much of the text did you understand?

90–100%:	10 points
70–90%:	8 points
50–70%:	5 points
20–40%:	2 points
below 20%:	0 points

Total (out of 40): _____

3 Great inventions: interview

Work with a partner. Each of you has invented something very important for the future of human life. Take turns to interview your partner about her/his invention.

Partner A: You have invented an anti-burglar device for houses.

Partner B: You have invented a new means of travel.

Take a few minutes to think about your invention before you start. How will it change people's lives?

Score
Give your partner up to 20 points for interesting ideas and details of invention.

Give up to 10 points each for fluency and accuracy.

Total (out of 40): _____

4 Take the floor

Work with a partner. Take it in turns to talk about your experiences on this course and your plans for afterwards. While one partner is speaking, the other partner should listen and time the speaker with a watch.

Score
Give your partner up to 10 points for each of the following:

Fluency
Accuracy
Interesting content
Length of time spoken (10 points for every minute without hesitation)

Total: _____

5 Grammar check

Tick the sentences which are correct. Put a cross by the sentences which contain mistakes and try to correct them.

a) Name cards must treat with respect.

b) Rules of etiquette must be followed carefully when doing business in Japan.

c) Give business contacts a present on their birthday is unusual in Britain.

d) Copies of all faxes sent must be kept in the file.

e) The earthquake has been made thousands of people homeless.

f) Many survivors have been found under the rubble.

g) By five o'clock yesterday afternoon the boy still had not been located.

h) By the end of last week we have seen no improvement in her health.

i) In the future there will be more old people.

j) Next year I think there would be a different party in government.

k) They said there would be plenty of food for everyone by the year 2050.

l) We will seen more people working from home in the next decade.

m) In 50 years' time the pollution of our rivers by factories will have been stopped.

n) By the end of next year 50 members of staff have been sacked.

o) I hoped that I will be invited to the party.

p) I was afraid of to become sick.

q) What you will be doing this time next year?

r) I hope I'll be working in Australia by then.

s) What time will you be leaving tonight?

t) She doesn't think she'll be living in the city in 20 years' time.

Score
Check your answers on page 90. Score 1 point for each correct tick or cross.

Score 2 points more for each corrected sentence.

Total: _____

Now add up your total score:

200–220	Brilliant!
160–199	Good.
120–159	Satisfactory.
80–119	Not bad, but don't forget to review the units regularly.
0–79	You definitely need to review Units 13-16 again.

B
Checklist

Tick if you are satisfied with your progress. Put a cross if you are not satisfied.

I can	yes/no
use passive constructions when talking and writing about the present and the past	
use passive constructions when talking and writing about the future	
talk about things that will happen in the future	
discuss my learning experiences	
use English confidently in most social situations	
speak English fluently for at least one minute without hesitating	

I know	yes/no
some useful information about social behaviour in different countries	
some set phrases for different social situations	
more about how to write good English	
more about how to understand English language radio and newspapers	
I have improved my speaking skills during this course	
I have improved my reading skills during this course	
I have improved my listening skillls during this course	
what my strengths and weaknesses in English are	
how to carry on learning after this course	

C
Personal plan

What problems do you have and how do you plan to help yourself?

Problems

_____

_____

Plans

_____

_____

ADDITIONAL
MATERIAL

Unit 8 Exercise 4

Group A story: What a shock!

It was a spring Sunday and therefore time for gardening. In a quiet suburb outside London, Jack got ready for an afternoon in the garden. Jack worked in a bank during the week but at weekends he loved gardening. He had his special gardening clothes: a green hat, a green jacket, and a pair of green rubber boots so his feet didn't get wet. He kept the gardening clothes in the big garage next to his house.

Jack spent a happy afternoon cutting the grass and planting seeds. At five o'clock he decided it was time for tea. He left the garden and walked to his garage. He put away his spade and other gardening tools in the garage. Then he started to change his clothes. He took off his hat and jacket and hung them up.

When he had done that, Jack started to walk to the house. Then he remembered that he had forgotten to change his boots. So he turned back to the garage.

Once he was back in the garage Jack started to take his boots off. The boots were rather tight and difficult to get off. Jack tried to pull off the right boot by pushing the right heel down with the toe of the left boot. It wasn't easy and Jack put out his hand to get support from the garage wall. By chance his hand was next to the light switch. Jack pushed down on the heel of his right boot with the toe of his left boot. He tried rocking forward and backwards to get the boot off.

It was in this position that a neighbour saw him. The neighbour saw Jack rocking forwards and backwards violently with his hand on the light switch. The neighbour thought he understood what was happening. Jack was getting an electric shock from the light switch. The neighbour quickly ran up, picked up the spade and smashed it down on Jack's arm. He wanted to get Jack away from the electricity! The blow broke Jack's arm in two places. Jack was very angry. He couldn't understand why his neighbour had attacked him.

Adapted from *The Guardian*

Unit 11 Exercise 4

Role descriptions

Student A

You are the Chair of the meeting. Your task is to start the discussion, to keep it going and to summarise at the end. You do not need to ask people to speak, or to control the discussion. You want to hear as many ideas as possible, so let the discussion take its own course. Only interrupt if the discussion seems to be stopping. A good way of keeping the discussion going is to ask each side to repeat points they have made so that everyone understands. Timing: check with the teacher, but aim for between 10 and 15 minutes.

Starting

Right, now that we're all here let's ...

OK, the topic for discussion this morning is ...

Who would like to say something about ...?

Keeping discussion going

Does everyone agree with that?

Would anyone like to come in here?

Could you please go over that again?

I'm not sure everyone got that. Could you go over it again, please?

Student B

You are an observer. Your role is to watch what happens during the meeting, take notes and then report back to the group and class at the end of the discussion. You do not say anything in the discussion. Take notes under these headings:

Language problems

Occasions when communication breaks down or the first language is used

Body language

The way people are sitting, the expression on their face, what they do with their hands

Who says what

Note who speaks most, and who listens to who.

Unit 8 Exercise 4

Group B story: Blue light means danger

The uncle of a friend of mine was driving home late one evening along a busy road. The thing is, though, that he was so tired he couldn't keep his eyes open and shouldn't really have been driving a car. He drove very, very slowly, swerving from one side of the motorway to the other. The other cars hooted at him and soon he could hear the 'na-na' of a police car behind him.

The police car stopped in front of my friend's uncle who managed to stop without running into it. Then he fell asleep. A policeman walked back from the police car and found my friend's uncle with his head on the steering wheel. 'OK, sir. We'd like you to leave your car and come to the police station with us,' the policeman said. My friend's uncle suddenly woke up and the police made him get out of his car.

At that moment there was a big crash on the opposite side of the motorway. Two cars had run into each other! 'Stay here!' the police shouted and ran across to the accident.

My friend's uncle saw his chance. He escaped and drove home as fast as he could. He put the car in the garage and locked the door. Then he ran into the house and said to his wife 'If the police come around I've been ill all day with a cold – I haven't been out and I haven't used the car.' Then he ran upstairs and went to bed.

Half an hour later the police arrived. The wife answered the door and said, 'He's been ill all day, he hasn't used the car, and he's asleep now' before the police asked anything.

'I see, madam,' one of the policemen said. 'Can we please look in your garage?'

When the policeman opened the garage door the wife got a surprise. There was the police car with the radio on and the blue light flashing.

Adapted from *The Guardian*

GRAMMAR REVIEW

Unit 1
1 Gerunds

The gerund is formed by adding 'ing' to the verb. It functions as a noun, and can be the subject or object of a sentence or come after a preposition.

Negatives: 'not' comes before the gerund.
    Not saying hello is rude.

There are three kinds of spelling change when forming the gerund.
1 If the verb ends in 'e', drop the 'e' before 'ing':
    dance – dancing
    If the verb ends in 'ee', make no change:
    see – seeing

2 If the verb has one syllable and ends in a vowel + a consonant, double the consonant before 'ing':
    put – putting; drop – dropping; run – running
    If the verb ends in 'y', 'w', or 'x', or in two consonants, or in two vowels, make no change:
    say – saying; push – pushing; look – looking

3 If the last syllable of a longer verb is stressed, double the consonant before 'ing':
    forget – forgetting

Use

Gerund as subject:
    Kissing the right cheek first is important.

Gerund as object:
    In some countries hand-shaking replaces *kissing*.

Gerund after preposition:
    You greet someone by *kissing*.

There are three categories of use after prepositions:
1 Verb + preposition + gerund
    I'm thinking about leaving.

    The gerund is used after these verbs and prepositions:
    agree with   put up with
    apologise for   rely on
    believe in   talk about
    feel like   think about.
    get on with

2 Adjective + preposition + gerund
    I'm keen on surfing.

    The gerund is used after these adjectives and prepositions:
    afraid of   grateful for
    annoyed with   interested in
    bad at   keen on
    bored with   responsible for
    fed up with   surprised at
    fond of   worried about
    good at   tired of

3 Preposition + gerund
    Before writing, read the question carefully.

    The gerund is used after these prepositions:
    after   in
    because of   on
    before   since
    by   what about
    for   with
    how about   without

Common errors

(x) I'm tired to watch TV.   (✔) I'm tired of watching TV.
(x) She's talking about to get divorced.   (✔) She's talking about getting divorced.
(x) How about to have a drink?   (✔) How about having a drink?

2 Question formation

'Yes/no' questions
A 'yes/no' question is a question which can be answered with 'yes' or 'no'.

Statement:
    Subject + auxiliary + verb
    You are going to Rio.

Question:
    Auxiliary + subject + verb
    Are you going to Rio?

The subject and auxiliary change places to form the question. When there is no auxiliary (present and past simple), 'do/does' or 'did' is added before the subject.

Statement:
    Subject + verb
    You live in Rio.

Question:
    Auxiliary + subject + verb
    Do you live in Rio?

'Wh-' questions
A 'wh-' question begins with: 'how', 'what', 'where', 'who', 'whose', 'when' or 'which'.
    'Wh-' question word + auxiliary + subject + verb
    Where are you going?

The subject and auxiliary change places after the 'wh-' question word. As with 'yes/no' questions 'do/does' or 'did' are added in the present and past simple.
    'Wh-' question word + auxiliary + subject + verb
    Where do you live?

'Wh-' questions with the verb 'be' have no auxiliary.
    'Wh-' question word + verb + subject
    Why are we late?
    Who is that?

Negative questions
A negative question is formed by putting 'not' or 'n't' in front of the auxiliary (or 'be' as main verb).
    Is it a nice day?   Isn't it a nice day?
    Do you want lunch?   Don't you want lunch?

Use
'Yes/no' questions
'Yes/no' questions are usually used to ask for information. They are also used for the following:
    Offering: Can I help you?
    Making requests: Can I have a coffee, please?
    Making suggestions: Can we do it this way?

'Wh-' questions
'**Who**' is always used for people. '**Which**' is used for people or things. '**What**' is usually used for things.
    Who is coming to the party?
    Which player scored the goal?
    Which seat do you want?
    What would you like to eat?

'**Which**' is used when there is a fixed number of possible answers. '**What**' is used when there is an unlimited number of answers.

'**Whose**' is used to ask 'belonging to which person?'.
    Whose hat is this?

'**Where**' is used to ask about place. '**When**' is used to ask about time. '**Why**' is used to ask for a reason.

'**How**' is used in three ways:
1 To ask about manner
    How do you get to Zanzibar? By ship.
2 Before adjectives or adverbs
    How old are you?
3 In greetings
    How are you?

Negative questions
Negative questions are used for the following:
1 To ask the listener to agree
    Isn't it a nice day?
2 To show surprise
    Aren't you ready yet?
3 To make a suggestion
    Why don't you wear a coat?

Common errors

(x) How much the cassette costs?   (✔) How much does the cassette cost?
(x) What means 'auxiliary'?   (✔) What does 'auxiliary' mean?
(x) Where you going?   (✔) Where are you going?

Unit 2
3 'Like' and 'would like'

The verb 'like' can be followed by either a gerund or an infinitive.
    The feeler is someone who likes reading.
    The feeler is someone who likes to read.

The conditional 'would like' has to be followed by an infinitive.
    The thinker is someone who would like to know everything there is to know.

'Like' is never used in the progressive.
    (x) I'm liking reggae.

'Like' always has an object, and adverbs follow the object.
    (x) I like a lot reading.   (✔) I like reading a lot.

Other verbs taking only the infinitive include:
    agree   hope
    ask   learn
    decide   offer
    expect   promise
    wish   refuse
    get

Other verbs taking only the gerund include:
    admit   imagine
    avoid   miss
    consider   practise
    deny   save
    finish   suggest

Use
Although 'like' can be followed by either a gerund or an infinitive with little change in meaning, the gerund is used more often to describe enjoying something, and the infinitive more often when a choice or habit is involved.
    I like travelling.
    I like to get up early.

Common errors

(x) Do you like having a drink? (= invitation)   (✔) Would you like to have a drink?
(x) Would you like going for a walk?   (✔) Would you like to go for a walk?
(x) I'm liking this film.   (✔) I like this film.
(x) She likes a lot computers.   (✔) She likes computers a lot.

Unit 3
4 'Used to'

'Used to' has no present or any other tense. It comes between the subject and main verb in a sentence.

Negatives: the negative is formed with the auxiliary 'did' and 'use'.

> I didn't use to eat meat.

Questions: questions are also formed with the auxiliary 'did'.

> Where did you use to play?

Use

'Used to' describes situations or habits in the past which no longer happen or exist.

> We used to sit together next to the stove.

'Would' can replace 'used to' but is more formal. 'Would' can only be used to describe past habits, not situations.

> I used to work all day/I would work all day.
> This building used to be a school.
> (x) This building would be a school.

Note the difference between 'used to' and 'be used to'. Compare:

> We used to sit by the stove. (then)
> We're used to sitting by the stove. (now)

'Be used to' is followed by the gerund or a noun and tells us about present habits, or things or situations which are familiar.

Common errors

(x) She uses to telephone every Sunday.	(✔) She telephones every Sunday or She used to telephone every Sunday.
(x) They were used to go home every weekend.	(✔) They used to go home every weekend.
(x) She usedn't to like fish.	(✔) She didn't use to like fish.
(x) Usedn't you to like ouzo?	(✔) Didn't you use to like ouzo?

5 Past simple: regular and irregular verbs

The past simple tense of regular verbs is formed by adding 'ed' to the verb (see the note on spelling below). For the past simple of irregular verbs see the irregular verb list on page 86.

I	**travelled**	to Germany when I was nine.
You	**learned**	Spanish in Barcelona.
She/he	**telephoned**	home yesterday.
It	**cleaned**	the car in five minutes.
We	**visited**	clothes shops all afternoon.
They	**lived**	in Hong Kong for three years.

Negatives: 'not' is added between subject and auxiliary verb 'did'.

> She didn't telephone her brother yesterday.

Questions: the auxiliary verb 'did' comes before the subject and the verb.

> Did she telephone her brother yesterday?

Note: there are three kinds of spelling change when forming the past simple of regular verbs:

1 If the verb ends in 'e' add 'd':
> smile – smiled

2 If the verb ends in 'y' drop the 'y' and add 'ied':
> study – studied

3 If the verb has one syllable and ends in a vowel and consonant, double the consonant before 'ed':
> pat – patted; drop – dropped

If the verb ends in 'w' or 'x', or in two or more consonants, or in a consonant after two vowels, make no change:
> tow – towed; push – pushed; cook – cooked

If the last syllable of a longer verb is stressed, double the final consonant:
> prefer – preferred

Use

The past simple is used to talk about events or circumstances at a fixed point in the past. It is also used to tell stories, for repeated actions and for states.

Story:	He **opened** the door quickly
Repeated action:	He **fired** three times.
State:	The room **smelled** of gunsmoke.

The past simple is often used with times, days and dates and with time expressions like:
> yesterday
> last month/year
> a day/week/month/year ago

Common errors

(x) He play music all night.	(✔) He played music all night.
(x) We goed to the party together.	(✔) We went to the party together.

6 Present perfect

The present perfect tense is formed with the auxiliary 'have' and the past participle of the verb. The past participle of regular verbs is formed with 'ed' in the same way as the past simple tense. For past participles of irregular verbs, see the irregular verb list on page 86.

	Subject + auxiliary + past participle	
I	**have lived**	here for ten years.
You	**have travelled**	abroad a lot.
She/he	**has been**	to the cinema.
It	**has worked**	well.
We	**have bought**	a new car.
They	**have been**	to Paris six times.

Negatives: 'not' is added between the auxiliary ('have/has') and the past participle.

> She hasn't been to the office.

Questions: the auxiliary verb ('have/has') comes before the subject and past participle.

> Has she been to the office?

Use

1 The present perfect links the past and the present. The past simple refers only to the past. Compare these sentences:

> I've just bought a new car. (I've still got it.)
> I bought a new car last week. (Perhaps I've still got it or perhaps I've sold it.)

> She's lived here for three years. (And still does.)
> She lived here for three years. (And then she moved.)

> He's had lots of different jobs. (And keeps on changing jobs.)
> He had lots of different jobs. (Before this one.)

2 The present perfect is often used on the radio and TV news and in newspapers to introduce a recent event (linking it with now) and the past simple is then used to give details of what happened.

> There has been a new development in the Australian hostage crisis. Three hostages escaped when armed police attacked the building.

3 The present perfect is often used with time expressions like:

already before	for
ever/never	since
just	

'For' and 'since' are often used with the negative present perfect.

> We haven't seen them for six months/since Christmas.

Common errors

(x) I've seen it yesterday.	(✔) I saw it yesterday.
(x) They know each other for years.	(✔) They've known each other for years.
(x) They have met three years ago.	(✔) They met three years ago.
(x) She has gone to Singapore on Friday.	(✔) She went to Singapore on Friday.

Unit 4
7 'Will' and 'going to' future

'Will'

The 'will' future is formed with 'will' and the infinitive without 'to'.

> Subject + 'will' + infinitive without 'to'
> She **will** (she'**ll**) **be** a millionaire in ten years' time.

Note: 'I' and 'we' can also be followed by 'shall' instead of 'will'.

Negatives: 'not' is added between the subject and 'will'.

> I hope it won't (will not) rain.

Questions: 'will' comes before the subject.

> Will you be late tonight?

'Going to'

The 'going to' future is formed with the verb 'be', 'going to' and the infinitive without 'to'.

> Subject + 'be' + 'going to' + infinitive without 'to'
> It'**s** (It **is**) **going to** rain.

Negatives: 'not' is added between 'be' and 'going'.

> It's not going to rain/It isn't going to rain.

Questions: 'be' comes before the subject.

> Is it going to rain?

Use

In addition to the uses described in Unit 4 on page 18, 'will' is often used for invitations, offers, promises and requests.

Invitation:	Will you have supper with us?
Offer:	I'll help you, if you like.
Promise:	I'll be home on time.
Request:	Will you deal with this, please?

Note: the present simple and present progressive can also be used to talk about the future. The present simple can be used when we are talking about timetables.

> We leave for the north on Monday.
> Her flight gets in at 6.

The present progressive can be used in a similar way to 'going to' to talk about future intentions and plans.

> She's returning to Poland on Tuesday.
> They're leaving for Malawi next week.

Common errors

(x) I help you with your work.	(✔) I'll help you with your work.
(x) I going to bed now.	(✔) I'm going to bed now.

Unit 5
8 Simple and first conditionals

Simple conditional

The simple conditional is formed in either of these two ways:

1 Present simple + 'if' + present simple
> main clause   'if'- clause
> People usually **respond** if you **ask** them for help.

2 'If' + present simple 'if'-clause + present simple main clause
> **If** there **is** a divorce, it **is** often the children who suffer.

As with all conditional sentences, the 'if'-clause can be before or after the main clause.

First conditional

The first conditional is formed with:

> 'If' + present simple 'if'-clause + main clause with 'will' + infinitive without 'to'
> **If** you **ask** them questions they **will** usually **try** to help.

Again, the order of the clauses can be reversed.

> They **will** usually **try** to help **if** you **ask** them questions.

Note: a modal (such as 'can' or 'may') or an imperative can be used in the main clause.

> If you are upset, tell someone.

Use

Simple conditional

This form is used to express a general truth. 'When' can replace 'if' with very little change in meaning.
  If you open the door, the house gets cold.
  When you open the door the house gets cold.

First conditional

This form is used to talk about possibilities. We don't know about the situation in the 'if'-clause, but it is possible that it will happen. The first conditional is sometimes called an open conditional because it leaves open the possibility in the 'if'-clause.
  If I remember, I'll telephone.

Common errors

- (x) If I'll see him I'll tell him.
- (✓) If I see him I'll tell him.
- (x) If I win the prize I give you a present.
- (✓) If I win the prize I'll give you a present.

Unit 6
9 Pointer words: 'this' and 'that'

Pointer words point to something which has been mentioned earlier (backward pointing) or to something which will be mentioned (forwards pointing).

'This' and 'that' are both used to point backwards.
  She was a woman. She was not bad-looking. She worked as a research scientist for Mars chocolate. All **this** made for easy headlines.

  I wanted to earn more money because I wanted to own a bigger flat and a faster car. **That** was what my life was about.

Only 'this' is used to point forwards.
  This is what we're going to do.

Note:
1 Plurals: this – these; that – those

2 'Here' can be used to replace 'this'. Radio and TV news broadcasts often begin 'Here is the six o'clock news …' and end 'That was the news at six o'clock'.

Unit 7
10 Second conditional

The second conditional is formed with:
  'If' + past simple 'if'-clause + main clause with 'would' + infinitive without 'to'
  If you **had** a problem, who **would** you **talk** to?
  He **wouldn't do** it **if** I **didn't nag** him.

Note:
1 The past continuous or 'could' can be used in the 'if'-clause instead of the past simple.
  If you were advising Kevin, what would you say?
  If you could choose a holiday anywhere in the world, where would you go?

2 'Were' is often used after 'if' instead of 'was', particularly when advice is given.
  If I were you, I wouldn't nag him.

Use

Although the second conditional uses past forms, it refers to the present or the future.

Present

If you had a problem, who would you talk to? (You don't have a problem now – we're talking about an unreal situation).

If I could make the laws, I would make burglars do hard physical labour. (I can't make the laws – we're talking about something unreal.)

Future

If I saved enough money, I would have a long holiday. (We're talking about a vague possibility in the future. It's much less definite than 'If I save enough money I'll have a long holiday'.)

Common errors

- (x) If I would have a car, I would give you a lift.
- (✓) If I had a car, I would give you a lift.
- (x) If you had telephoned, you will know I was busy.
- (✓) If you had telephoned, you would know I was busy.

Unit 8
11 Past progressive

The past progressive is formed with 'was/were' and the 'ing' form of the verb.
  I/he/she/it **was standing**
  You/we/they **were standing**

See Grammar Review 1 for spelling of the 'ing' form.

Negatives: 'not' comes between 'was/were' and the 'ing' form.
  I was not listening.

Questions: 'was/were' comes before the subject.
  Were they waiting?

Use

1 The past progressive refers to a past event or situation which had started but not finished. It is often used to describe the background when we tell stories.
  The manager was standing in the supermarket doorway when the trolley hit him on the knee. (The background is the longer action of the manager standing in the doorway so this is in the past progressive. The shorter completed action of the trolley hitting him is in the past simple.)

2 The past progressive is also used to describe something that was in progress throughout a period of time.
  It was very quiet so we were always looking for ways to liven things up.

Note: some verbs are not usually used in the progressive form. We can say 'I liked the film', but not 'I was liking the film'. Here are 22 of those verbs:

agree	like/dislike	smell
believe	love	sound
disagree	need	taste
forget	prefer	think (= believe)
hate	remember	understand
hear	see	want
know	seem	wish

Common errors

- (x) I was believing you weren't coming.
- (✓) I believed you weren't coming.
- (x) She was wanting to speak to him.
- (✓) She wanted to speak to him.
- (x) The cook tried the soup to see how it was tasting.
- (✓) The cook tried the soup to see how it tasted.

12 Past perfect

The past perfect is formed with 'had' and the past participle.
  Subject + 'had' + past participle
  The parcel **had arrived**.

Negatives: 'not' comes between 'had' and the past participle.
  It had not arrived.

Questions: 'had' comes before the subject.
  Had it arrived?

Note: see page 86 for irregular verb past participles.

Use

1 The past perfect is used when we are talking about a past event and want to refer to something which happened even earlier in the past.
  This was when I was 19 and had met my dream man. (At the time of the story the speaker was aged 19. Before the time of the story she met her dream man.)

2 The past perfect is often used after verbs of saying and thinking. See Grammar Review 13.
  He told them/thought that the bus had left.

Common errors

- (x) When I got there the party already started.
- (✓) When I got there the party had already started.
- (x) She knew she met them before.
- (✓) She knew she had met them before.

Unit 9
13 Reported speech

In reporting what someone said, verbs in the present tense are changed into the past.

Direct speech	Reported speech
'I do.'	She said she **did**.
'I'm leaving.'	He said he **was** leaving.

Verbs in the past change into the past perfect.
| 'We played squash' | He said they **had played** squash. |

Note:
1 Verbs already in the past perfect do not change.

2 Past forms of modal verbs:
can – could	will – would,
may – might	(must – had to)
shall – should	

3 Pointer words and words referring to the time and place of speech often change.
this – that	tomorrow – the next day
now – then	yesterday – the previous day
here – there	
I'll see you tomorrow	She said she would see him the next day.

Note the following exceptions:
1 If 'says' instead of 'said' is used as the reporting verb, there is no tense change.
  It's time to go.   She says it's time to go.

2 If we are reporting something that is true now, or is a general fact, a tense change is not necessary.
  The capital of Namibia is Windhoek.   She said the capital of Namibia is Windhoek.

14 Question tags

Question tags are formed with a pronoun and an auxiliary verb. Negative question tags usually follow positive statements.
  + 　　　　　　　　 -
  You like me,　　 don't you?

Positive question tags usually follow negative statements.
  -　　　　　　　　　 +
  You didn't go there,　did you?

When the statement uses the verb 'be' or an auxiliary verb, this is used in the question tag.
  You're leaving now, aren't you?
  It's difficult, isn't it?
  You can tell me, can't you?
  You'll write to me, won't you?

If the statement is in the present simple, 'do' is used in the question tag. If the statement is in the past simple, 'did' is used.
  They want to come, don't they?
  She got the job, didn't she?

Note:
1 Positive question tags can also follow positive statements with a change in meaning. See 'Use' below.
  So you're leaving, are you?

2 The question tag for 'I am' is 'aren't I?'
  I'm next, aren't I?

Use

1 A question tag is usually an invitation to agree with a statement or a way of checking information. If we are asking for agreement, a falling intonation is used in the tag. If we are checking information, a rising intonation is used in the tag.

2 A positive question tag after a positive statement is often used to react to something someone has said.
  So it's time to go, is it?
  The reaction can be one of pleasure, but often shows a negative attitude.
  So you think you're clever, do you?

Common errors

- (x) You didn't see them, didn't you?
- (✓) You didn't see them, did you?
- (x) She was there, isn't it?
- (✓) She was there, wasn't she?

Unit 10
15 Modal auxiliaries

The modal auxiliaries 'might', 'may', 'must' and 'should' come between the subject and the infinitive without 'to'.

I/you/he/she/it/we/they	**might**	be right.
	may	
	must	
	should	

Negatives: 'not' comes between the modal auxiliary and the main verb.

    You should not experiment on animals.

Questions: the modal auxiliary comes before the subject.

    Might gene transplants save lives?

Use

1 'May' and 'might' both refer to possibility. 'Might' refers to something which is less likely or possible than 'may'.

    It may rain tomorrow. (We don't know but there is a possibility.)

    It might rain tomorrow. (We don't know but there a slight possibility.)

2 'May' and (rarely) 'might' are also used when talking about permission. They are more polite and formal than 'can' and 'could'. 'May' is used to ask for and give permission in formal situations.

    May I open the window?

    Yes, you may.

3 'Must' and 'should' are both used to express obligation. 'Must' is stronger than 'should'. Compare:

    You must not drink and drive. (It's against the law.)

    You shouldn't smoke. (It's not healthy.)

4 'Must' and 'have to' are also used to describe being certain about something.

    It must be supper-time. I'm so hungry.

    'Should' is used to describe being almost certain about something.

    Supper should be ready soon. I put it on to cook an hour ago.

Common errors

(**x**) She must to leave now.	(✔) She must leave now.
(**x**) You should stopping it.	(✔) You should stop it.

Unit 11
16 Conjunctions and connectors

Use

'Although', 'however, 'nevertheless' and 'on the other hand' are used to link two different or contrasting ideas. ('Although' is a conjunction like 'but', 'and', 'because', 'so', 'whereas' etc.), joining the ideas together to form a single sentence.

    He wants a new camera. However, he can't afford one.

    Although he wants a new camera, he can't afford one.

Other conjunctions and connectors include:

1 'and', 'moreover', 'also': used to link ideas without contrast.

    He wants a new camera and he can easily afford one.

2 'or', 'either . . . or': used to give alternatives

    Either we buy him a camera or he'll go out and steal one!

3 'so', 'therefore': used to show a result

    He earned some extra money, so he bought himself a camera.

17 Prepositions of time

Use

1 '**At**' is used to state a fixed time and before short holidays:

at nine thirty	at lunchtime
at midnight	at the weekend
at New Year	

It is also used in these expressions:

at night	at the moment
	at the same time

2 '**On**' is used with days and dates:

on my birthday	on June 9th
on Saturday	

3 '**In**' is used with longer periods of time:

in June	in 1996
in the summer	

It is also used with parts of the day and to talk about a period of time in the future:

    in the morning/afternoon/evening

    in nine months' time

    in a few minutes

4 '**By**' is used when we mean 'not later than':

    Be home by ten o'clock. (= Be home at or before ten o'clock.)

5 '**For**' is used to show the length of a period of time:

for ten years	for five minutes
for a week	

6 '**For**' and '**since**' are often used with the present perfect tense. 'For' is used before a period of time and 'since' to show the start of a period.

    She hasn't had a cigarette for ten years.

    She hasn't had a cigarette since 1986.

Common errors

(**x**) on the morning	(✔) in the morning
(**x**) I've been here since three hours	(✔) I've been here for three hours
(**x**) on Christmas	(✔) at Christmas

Unit 12
18 Present simple passive

The present simple passive is formed with the present simple tense of the verb 'be' and the past participle.

    Subject + 'be' + past participle + 'by' + agent

    Evaluation **is shown** by a closed hand.

Often 'by' + agent can be left out.

    The hand **is used** to cover the mouth.

Negatives: 'not' comes after 'be' and before the past participle.

    The weather is not expected to change.

Questions: 'be' comes before the subject.

    Is the train expected soon?

    When is the train expected?

Use

The passive is used to put information we wish to emphasise at the start of the sentence. The passive is used most frequently in written English and in formal situations. It is often used to describe processes and rules.

'By' + agent is left out when the agent is obvious or not known. In the example given above it is not necessary to write 'The hand is used to cover the mouth by people' because we know that the writer is writing about people.

When verbs stand on their own without an object (intransitive verbs), they cannot be used in the passive. For example, 'The bus leaves at nine' cannot be turned into a passive sentence. Other verbs which also cannot be used in the passive include 'be', 'have' and 'seem'.

Common errors

(**x**) A new car is had by her.	(✔) She has a new car.
(**x**) When is expected the plane?	(✔) When is the plane expected?

Unit 13
19 Passive with modals

The passive used with modal verbs ('can', 'could', 'may', 'might', 'will', 'would', 'shall', 'should', 'must', 'ought') is formed in the same way as the present simple passive.

    Subject + modal + 'be' + past participle

    Name cards **must be treated** with respect.

Negatives: 'not' comes after the modal and before 'be'.

    The giving and receiving of a card must not be done at the same time.

Questions: the modal comes before the subject.

    Should name cards be printed in English and Japanese?

Note: the passive is formed similarly after 'have to', 'going to', 'want to', and 'would like to'.

    It has to be cooked slowly.

    It's going to be delivered tomorrow.

    They want to be met at the station.

    She would like to be treated with respect.

Use

The passive used with modal verbs emphasises what is done to the subject.

    The name card should be presented with two hands.

Common errors

(**x**) The card should to be held like this.	(✔) The card should be held like this.
(**x**) Presenting cards must be doing correctly.	(✔) Presenting cards must be done correctly.

20 Past simple passive

The past simple passive is formed in the same way as the present simple passive, using the past simple instead of the present simple.

    Subject + 'was/were' + past participle (+ 'by' + agent)

    The winner of the games **was announced**.

Use

The past simple passive is used in the same way as the present simple passive.

Note: both present and past simple passive can be used with 'it' + a reporting verb.

    'It' + 'be' + 'that' + clause

    It was said that the professor was very angry.

Reporting verbs include:

agree	report
believe	request
decide	say
expect	see
feel	suppose
hope	think
know	understand

Common errors

(**x**) Frank was to be told it was a summer party.	(✔) Frank was told it was a summer party.
(**x**) A lot of wine was drinking.	(✔) A lot of wine was drunk.

Unit 14
21 Present perfect passive

The present perfect passive is formed on the same model as the other passives, using the present perfect form of 'be'.
> Subject + 'has/have been' + past participle
> + 'by' + agent
> At least ten people **have been killed** by floods.

Negatives: 'not' comes after 'has/have' and before 'been'.
> Rescuers have not been supplied with equipment.

Questions: 'has/have' comes before the subject.
> Has everything been done to help the survivors?

Use

The present perfect passive is often used in newspapers and on radio and TV news broadcasts. Like the present perfect, it provides a link between past events and now and is usually followed by a more detailed description of events in the past simple. Frequently in newspapers or news broadcasts use of the present perfect passive means that we hear first about the effect or result of some action rather than about the agent that caused it.
> Thousands have been made homeless by floods.
> Three hostages have been freed by police.

Common errors

(x) A movie star is been found dead.	(✔) A movie star has been found dead.
(x) Did everything been eaten?	(✔) Has everything been eaten?

22 Past perfect passive

The past perfect passive is formed like the present perfect passive, using 'had been' before the past participle.
> Subject + 'had been' + past participle (+ 'by' + agent)
> Mrs Kim **had been saved** by rescue boats.

Negatives: 'not' comes after 'had' and before 'been'.
> The tragedy had not been expected.

Questions: 'had' comes before the subject.
> Had the bridge been checked before it collapsed?

Use

See Grammar Review 12 on the past perfect. The past perfect passive is used in the same way, but puts emphasis on the effect or result of an action rather than the agent that caused it.

Common error

(x) Questions had been asking in parliament.	(✔) Questions had been asked in parliament.

Unit 15
23 Future passive

The future passive is formed in the same way as the other passives with 'will be' and the past participle.
> Subject + 'will' + 'be' + past participle (+ 'by' + agent)
> Balloons **will be guided** by wire from city to city.

Negatives: 'not' comes after 'will' and before 'be'.
> Cars will not be powered by petrol.

Questions: 'will' comes before the subject.
> Will cars still be needed?

Note: 'is/are going to' can be substituted for 'will' with the same difference in meaning as in active sentences.

Use

The future passive tells us about future events even though it uses the past participle of the main verb.

24 Future perfect passive

The future perfect is formed with 'will have' and the past participle.
> Subject + 'will' + 'have' + past participle
> She **will have got** the message.

The future perfect passive is formed with 'will have been' and the past participle.
> Subject + 'will' + 'have' + 'been' + past participle
> Disease **will have been wiped** out.

Negatives: 'not' comes after 'will'.
> Disease will not have been wiped out.

Questions: 'will' comes before the subject.
> Will disease have been wiped out?

Use

The future perfect is sometimes called the past in the future. It is used to refer to an event which will happen in the future before a time which is even further in the future.

Common error

(x) By 2050 much of the rainforest will destroy by humans.	(✔) By 2050 much of the rainforest will have been destroyed by humans.

Unit 16
25 Future progressive

The future progressive is formed with 'will be' and the present participle.
> Subject + 'will' + 'be' + present participle
> I **will be working** abroad.

Negatives: 'not' comes after 'will' and before 'be'.
> I won't be living here any more.

Questions: 'will' comes before the subject.
> Will you still be working here?

Use

The future progressive is used to refer to something happening at a point in the future.

1 It is used for events which will be routine in the future:
> I'll be working abroad.
> I'll be living in Hungary.

2 It is used for events which are already planned or to predict them:
> I'll be leaving at six o'clock.
> She'll be returning on the 29th.

3 It is also sometimes used to make polite requests for information about what people are planning to do:
> Will you be staying long?
> Will you be using the car this evening? (Because if you won't, I will!)

Common error

(x) This time next year I'm travelling in Africa.	(✔) This time next year I'll be travelling in Africa.

IRREGULAR VERBS

Verb	Past simple	Past participle	Verb	Past simple	Past participle
awake	awoke	awoken	light	lit, lighted	lit, lighted
be	was, were	been	lose	lost	lost
beat	beat	beaten	make	made	made
become	became	become	mean	meant	meant
begin	began	begun	meet	met	met
bend	bent	bent	mistake	mistook	mistaken
bet	bet, betted	bet, betted	misunderstand	misunderstood	misunderstood
bite	bit	bitten	overcome	overcame	overcome
bleed	bled	bled	overtake	overtook	overtaken
blow	blew	blown	pay	paid	paid
break	broke	broken	put	put	put
bring	brought	brought	read	read	read
build	built	built	ride	rode	ridden
burn	burnt, burned	burnt, burned	ring	rang	rung
burst	burst	burst	rise	rose	risen
buy	bought	bought	run	ran	run
can	could	was able	say	said	said
catch	caught	caught	see	saw	seen
choose	chose	chosen	sell	sold	sold
come	came	come	send	sent	sent
cost	cost	cost	set	set	set
cut	cut	cut	sew	sewed	sewn, sewed
dig	dug	dug	shake	shook	shaken
do	did	done	shine	shone	shone
draw	drew	drawn	shoot	shot	shot
dream	dreamt, dreamed	dreamt, dreamed	show	showed	shown
drink	drank	drunk	shut	shut	shut
drive	drove	driven	sing	sang	sung
eat	ate	eaten	sink	sank	sunk
fall	fell	fallen	sit	sat	sat
feed	fed	fed	sleep	slept	slept
feel	felt	felt	slide	slid	slid
fight	fought	fought	smell	smelt, smelled	smelt, smelled
find	found	found	speak	spoke	spoken
fly	flew	flown	spell	spelt, spelled	spelt, spelled
forbid	forbad	forbidden	spend	spent	spent
forecast	forecast	forecast	spin	span	spun
forget	forgot	forgotten	split	split	split
forgive	forgave	forgiven	spoil	spoilt, spoiled	spoilt, spoiled
freeze	froze	frozen	spread	spread	spread
get	got	got	stand	stood	stood
give	gave	given	steal	stole	stolen
go	went	gone	stick	stuck	stuck
grow	grew	grown	strike	struck	struck
hang	hung, hanged	hung, hanged	swear	swore	sworn
have	had	had	swim	swam	swum
hear	heard	heard	take	took	taken
hide	hid	hidden	teach	taught	taught
hit	hit	hit	tear	tore	torn
hold	held	held	tell	told	told
hurt	hurt	hurt	think	thought	thought
keep	kept	kept	throw	threw	thrown
know	knew	known	understand	understood	understood
lay	laid	laid	upset	upset	upset
lead	led	led	wake	woke	woken
learn	learnt, learned	learnt, learned	wear	wore	worn
leave	left	left	weep	wept	wept
lend	lent	lent	win	won	won
let	let	let	write	wrote	written
lie	lay	lain			

ANSWER KEY

Unit 1 Exercise 1(a)

American 1	Argentinian 8
Brazilian 3	British 2
Egyptian 9	German 5
Indonesian 7	Russian 4
South Africa 6	

Unit 1 Exercise 1(b)

Arabic 8	French 6
English 9	Italian 7
German 3	Spanish 5
Japanese 4	Portuguese 1
Chinese 2	

Unit 1 Exercise 2(e)

stroking his/her upper arm
tapping his/her shoulder or back
patting his/her cheeks
squeezing his/her hands
poking his chest
bumping into a friend
joining a group
walking into a party
greeting your friend

Unit 1 Exercise 3

1 In south-west Nigeria it is wrong to ask how many children someone has.
2 Correct
3 In Vietnam it is rude to ask if someone is married.
4 In parts of Nigeria it is OK to ask how much someone earns.
5 Correct

Unit 1 Exercise 4(c)

The weather, the flight, food, borrowing something to read, the time, the journey, the news and current affairs.

Unit 2 Exercise 3(a)

Angela: grammar, pronunciation
Yuko: vocabulary, speaking
Hiromi: speaking
Sven: reading, writing
Jacek: listening, speaking
Yves: speaking, review

Unit 3 Exercise 1(a)

a) 2	d) 3	f) 7
b) 5	e) 1	g) 4
c) 6		

Unit 4 Exercise 1(b)

1 (d)	3 (b)
2 (a)	4 (c)

Unit 4 Exercise 1(c)

Fly to South Africa	4
Start university	8
Have a holiday in Malta	1
Visit Malawi	6
Go to Zimbabwe	5
Get a job	3
Live in Italy	2
Travel to Zanzibar	7

Review 1 Exercise 2

a) true	e) true	h) true
b) false	f) false	i) false
c) true	g) true	j) true
d) false		

Review 1 Exercise 3

a) Not very happy. They found it too hot and worried about how they would survive it.
b) The fact that they were surrounded by black people who were lawyers and doctors etc., and that they were with strong, positive women who didn't think their place was in the kitchen. This gave them a positive image of themselves as black women. Also, the music probably influenced Des'ree's choice of career.
c) Because Des'ree made up songs and sang them to imaginary audiences. She had a very positive attitude. Her friends liked her *Dallas* song.
d) Yes. They sat together all day in the mango tree and shared secrets. Esther enjoyed Des'ree's songs and pretend performances and felt protective towards her.

Review 1 Exercise 5

a) X Do you know what the time is?
b) ✓
c) X You're going to Rio, aren't you?
d) ✓
e) X What do you think about this book?
f) X I don't need to learn writing in English.
g) ✓
h) X Why are you learning English? ('Why do you learn English?' is not incorrect in some circumstances.)
i) X My mother used to play with me all day.
j) ✓
k) ✓
l) X I was sick yesterday.
m) X They have lived here for six years.
n) ✓
o) ✓
p) ✓
q) X I expect I'll become very rich one day / I hope I become very rich one day.
r) X I'd like to go to college next year.
s) ✓
t) ✓

Unit 5 Exercise 2(d)

The sound of the phone	5
Laughing at mother	1
Waiting to make a call	3
Solving the problem	6
Having to make a call	2
Closing the door	4

Unit 5 Exercise 2(e)

1 scream	5 snap
2 cry	6 growl
3 roar	7 croak
4 bark	

Unit 5 Exercise 2(f)

1 the telephone
2 the door
3 the dog
4 the person who phoned
5 this knowledge

Unit 5 Exercise 3(d)

1 it's best to tell someone if you think it will help.
2 you let them know what's happening.
3 they will usually try to help.
4 if you see your other parent.

Unit 5 Exercise 4

1 true	5 true	9 true
2 true	6 true	10 true
3 true	7 true	
4 true	8 true (Denmark is first)	

Unit 6 Exercise 1(a)

1 Boris Yeltsin
2 Mother Teresa
3 Mao Zedong
4 Winnie Mandela

Unit 6 Exercise 2(d)

Helen was born in 1954. She became Britain's first and only astronaut. Now someone has written a book about her. The book describes her unusual childhood and family background. Helen believes that people are interested in space travel because they want to know how the world began. She went to live in Russia because she wanted a bigger flat and a faster car. However, she found that although Russian families were larger, their flats were not. Money used to be important for her but it is no longer. Helen believes in God and votes conservative. The first astronauts had to be very brave. But now anyone can become an astronaut if they are hard-working enough.

Unit 6 Exercise 3(a)

1 background
2 familiar
3 fascinated
4 reveals
5 single
6 dependants
7 aspire to
8 zing (colloquial word)
9 laid-back
10 brave

Unit 6 Exercise 3(c)

Any of the following are possible:

matter-of-fact	straightforward
boring	intelligent
realistic	open-minded
thoughtful	relaxed
hard-working	sensible

Unit 6 Exercise 3(d)

1 'I wanted to earn more money because I wanted a bigger flat and a faster car'
2 'family and friends'
3 'your hi-fi ... your washing machine or your microwave'
4 how she voted in the last election
5 'all this' = the world and space

Unit 7 Exercise 3

Suggested answers

Expressions with 'get'
1 Don't let it upset you.
2 You really don't understand …
3 What do you mean?/What are you trying to say?
4 We made a bad start to our relationship, didn't we?
5 I really love …
6 He began a romantic relationship with my friend …
7 You'll recover/feel better one day.
8 Let's start!
9 It's getting late.
10 We contacted/called the police immediately.

Expressions with 'go'
1 I'm doing everything in my power to get promotion.
2 He didn't agree with the plan.
3 She broke her promise.
4 This will be remembered as the most exciting match of the year.
5 It was uncertain that it would succeed.
6 He attacked him with a knife.
7 I don't want to talk about it in detail now.
8 I'm going mad!

Unit 7 Exercise 4

Suggested answers

Conversation 1: (e)
Conversation 2: (b)
Conversation 3: (c)

Unit 8 Exercise 2

First caller
c) Me and my three friends, Neil, Peter and Richard, were standing
    Neil was holding
    Richard and I were carrying
    The manager was standing

Second caller
b) 1 false (in London)
    2 true
    3 true
    4 false (Ralph did.)
    5 true
    6 false (He took another woman.)
    7 false (She bought four mice.)
    8 true

c) I had never known
    he had arranged
    I'd done well
    who had driven
    Ralph had taken
    he had lied … and had taken
    the mice had eaten
    the mice had dug … and had damaged

Unit 8 Exercise 3

OK, Derek, let's hear all about it.
Uh-huh.
Winner of what?
Really?
Do go on.
So how did it end?
So let's hear what happened.
I see.
Yes …?
What happened next?

Review 2 Exercise 2

a) 1   c) 1   e) 1
b) 2   d) 3

Review 2 Exercise 5

a) ✔
b) X She said goodbye to him.
c) ✔
d) X My daughter started school last week.
e) X If you are upset, tell someone.
f) ✔
g) X If it rains you will need an umbrella.
h) ✔
i) ✔
j) X I would be sad if I didn't see you again.
k) X They wouldn't like it if you didn't come.
l) X He was thinking about her when she called.
m) ✔
n) X I couldn't open the door because I had left the key in my other jacket.
o) ✔
p) X Fred was walking down the road when suddenly he was attacked by some hooligans.
q) ✔
r) ✔
s) X I felt sad that my parents had divorced.
t) ✔

Unit 9 Exercise 2(a)

Yale says that he and Mary 'cut it off' – this means that they ended the relationship.

Yale suggests that Ike calls Mary – that he telephones her.

Ike says that Yale is crazy. He says that he can't call Mary as he still thinks of Yale and Mary as being together.

Unit 9 Exercise 2(b)

Ike kisses Mary.

Unit 9 Exercise 2(d)

Conversation (a): 'I – I should call her?'
'She said she found me attractive?'
Conversation (b): Mary means that she knew that Ike wanted to kiss her.
Conversation (c): Mary says, 'There's something I – I want to tell you.'

Unit 10 Exercise 2(a)

1 $2bn world-wide project leads torrent of breakthroughs
2 Frankenfood hits the menus
3 Race to design pigs that live on grass
4 Baby to get first gene transplant. Operation aims to cure rare immune system deficiency
5 'Human' hearts bred in pigs for transplants

Unit 10 Exercise 3(b)

Jeff Sachs
1 I believe that we experiment on animals because they are powerless to stop us, and we count their pain as unimportant when measured agaisnt our own interests.
2 It's not that we think animals can't feel pain – we know very well that they do.
3 And it's dangerous to say that we use animals in experiments because they lack our intelligence.
4 Is it right to kill one human being in an experiment to save thousands of others?

Dr Clark
1 Is Jeff arguing that we must all become vegetarians and stop eating meat?
2 Does Jeff want humans to die to save the lives of animals?
3 Is Jeff against animal research to find cures for sick animals?
4 If he isn't, why is it wrong to do the same experiments to find cures for sick people?

Unit 11 Exercise 1(c)

Journalist

Unit 11 Exercise 2(a)

There are no definite answers but these are some of the functions the lists might contain:

Hotel receptionist
Listening and speaking:

phone calls
supplying information
giving directions
dealing with complaints
taking bookings
receiving guests
offering help and advice
taking payment

Reading and writing:

faxes and telexes
booking letters
hotel information

Secretary in an international company
Listening and speaking:

phone calls
greeting visitors
making travel and other arrangements
supplying information
offering help and advice

Reading and writing:

faxes and telexes
business letters
brochures and company information
programmes for visitors
instructions

Tour guide
Listening and speaking:

supplying information
answering questions
describing events and places
making arrangements
giving talks
making bookings
dealing with complaints

Reading and writing:

guidebooks
letters confirming arrangements

Sales representative for an international company
Listening and speaking:

giving talks
explaining how things work
discussing prices and contracts
making travel arrangements
socialising

Reading and writing:

brochures
instructions
business letters
contracts
price lists
specifications

Unit 11 Exercise 2(c)

Suggested answers

1 two weeks ago/when he had a visit from two representatives from Bristol/when he had English visitors.
2 meets an Englishman.
3 afraid of saying something wrong.
4 he meets people from other countries.
5 there are several people present.

Unit 11 Exercise 5(a)

Suggested answers for UK/USA

1 T	4 B	7 T
2 T	5 B	8 T
3 L	6 B	9 L

Unit 12 Exercise 2(a)

1 Hearing, seeing or speaking a lie, paragraph (c)
2 Covering mouth, paragraph (i)
3 Rubbing eye, paragraph (h)
4 Rubbing ear, paragraph (b)
5 Scratching neck, paragraph (g)
6 Sucking, paragraph (f)
7 Boredom, paragraph (a)
8 Evaluation, paragraph (e)
9 Stroking chin, paragraph (d)

Unit 12 Exercise 3(a)

1 work	5 look	9 treat
2 speak	6 give	10 make
3 vary	7 pause	
4 present	8 summarise	

Unit 12 Exercise 3(b)

1 contact	7 bored
4 questions	8 still
5 feelings	9 conversation
6 clarification	10 end

Review 3 Exercise 1

a) true	f) false	k) true
b) true	g) true	l) true
c) false	h) false	m) true
d) false	i) true	n) true
e) true	j) true	o) true

Review 3 Exercise 3

a) This
b) in fact/so
c) first of all/for instance/in fact
d) such as
e) furthermore/in addition/in fact
f) lastly
g) however
h) in addition/so
i) on the other hand/however
j) however/for instance
k) for instance/however/on the other hand
l) so

Review 3 Exercise 5

a) ✔
b) ✔
c) X Mimi did arrive on time, didn't she?/Mimi didn't arrive on time, did she?
d) X You would like being called 'Ducks', wouldn't you?/You like being called 'Ducks', don't you?
e) ✔
f) X The BBC said that divorce was increasing in the UK.
g) X I must go home right away.
h) ✔
i) X Due to the fact that he was late, the dinner was spoiled./Because he was late .../As he was late ...
j) X Although he had many affairs, they didn't get divorced.
k) ✔
l) X On the one hand, he is a good actor, but on the other hand he's not very good-looking, is he?
m) X The director said he would see you on Monday at noon.

n) ✔
o) ✔
p) ✔ (Note: 'on the weekend' is American usage.)
q) ✔
r) X The equipment is used all day long by the visitors to the gym.
s) ✔
t) X What sort of food is eaten in Thailand?

Unit 13 Exercise 2(a)

1 Hong Kong
2 Hong Kong
3 exporter
4 America
5 buyer

Unit 13 Exercise 2(c)

Mr Richardson
1 Pleased about the meeting.
2 Happy that he and Mr Chu are using first names.
3 Thinks that Mr Chu is friendly and easy to do business with.
4 Looks forward to meeting again.

Mr Chu
1 Not pleased about the meeting.
2 Uncomfortable with Mr Richardson.
3 Thinks that Mr Richardson does not understand cultural differences.
4 Does not look forward to meeting again.

Unit 13 Exercise 4(a)

Suggested answers

1 on time.
2 a present (for the host).
3 introduce yourself to all the other guests.
4 raise your glass, look everyone in the eye, empty your glass and look everyone in the eye again before putting down your glass.

Unit 13 Exercise 4(b)

He arrived on time and brought the professor a bunch of flowers
Frank was introduced to the other guests
there was a great deal of conversation
it was the professor
She was thrown into the swimming pool
After that everyone went home

Unit 13 Exercise 4(c)

Suggested answers

He arrived late and had left the bunch of flowers on the bus
Frank introduced himself to the other guests
there was no conversation
it was Frank
He was thrown into the swimming pool
After that there was hot coffee and more singing and dancing

Unit 13 Exercise 5

Suggested answers

1 How do you do?
2 – (There is no set phrase for starting a meal, although waiters in restaurants often say 'Enjoy your meal'.)
3 Happy New Year!
4 Many happy returns!/Happy birthday!
5 Cheers! (You also hear this used instead of 'Good-bye'.)
6 Congratulations!
7 I'm so sorry. That's terrible.
8 Best of luck!
9 I hope you feel better soon.
10 Bless you!

Unit 14 Exercise 2(a)

1 a) Holland b) A large store c) Snakes to guard jewels d) The next four weeks
2 a) London b) Linda Essex c) To marry for 16th time d) Today
3 a) New York b) Picasso painting c) Sold for $3.2 million d) Yesterday
4 a) California b) Scott Palmer c) Has had 18 holes in one d) Since 1983

Unit 14 Exercise 4(a)

Suggested answers

Possible headlines
1 100 feared dead in Italian floods
Italian floods claim up to 100 lives
2 Seoul bridge collapse
32 dead in bridge horror
Mayor resigns after bridge tragedy

Possible shortened versions of the texts
1 At least 50 people have been killed and thousands made homeless during the worst rainstorms to hit north-west Italy in 80 years.
    Rescuers have been searching for 12 people missing in the countryside around the city of Turin but with little hope of finding them alive.
    Italian TV forecast that the death toll could rise as high as 100 when floodwaters went down. 'The official figure is 35 dead and about a dozen missing,' said Ombretta Fumagilli Carulli, Under-Secretary for Civil Protection. 'But we can say with certainty that the number of victims will rise.'
(95 words)

2 The mayor of Seoul resigned after at least 32 people were killed and 17 injured when a bridge in the centre of the capital collapsed.
    Commuters watched in horror as the central part of the four-lane Songsu bridge plunged into the Han river taking with it cars, vans, and a full bus. 'How could a bridge which millions use every day collapse so easily?' said a schoolteacher, Kim Min-ja, who had been saved by rescue boats.
    Only recently questions have been asked in parliament about the safety of the 17 bridges which cross the Han in Seoul.
(97 words)

Unit 14 Exercise 5(b)

Broadcast

1 The Queen:	has been arrested
2 The weather:	hot and dry
3 Switzerland:	the civil war in Zurich continues
4 Finance:	the drouble has been revalued

Unit 15 Exercise 1(a)

telephone (1872–6), motor car (1885), railways (1829)

The dates of invention of the others are:
television (1926)
aeroplane (1903)
vacuum cleaner (1907)
washing machine (1907)
radio (1901)

Unit 15 Exercise 3

The descriptions of William Henry Hoover and the Earl of Sandwich are true.

Review 4 Exercise 1

It is important to realise that the Fijians' culture dictates
that they should always invite a stranger into their
home, whether they can afford to feed that stranger
or not. Before the visit, if you have the opportunity,
buy a kilo of *kava* root from an outdoor market. It is a
traditional gift. Your host will gladly accept the gift and
may perform a welcoming ritual that says your visit is
officially recognised by the village. You will be offered
a drink of *yaqona*, which, of course, you should accept
and drink in one big gulp rather than in sips. When
invited inside a *bure*, remove your shoes. Place them
outside the door and stoop slightly when entering. Avoid
standing fully upright indoors. It's bad manners. Dress
modestly when visiting a village. Men should not be
bare-chested and women should wear trousers or a long
dress and definitely not shorts or a bathing suit. When
entering a village, take off your hat.

kava root = the root of a kind of pepper plant (the *kava*)
            which is important in Fijian culture
yaqona   = a special drink made from *kava* root used for
            rituals and ceremonies
bure   = a Fijian home or hut

Review 4 Exercise 2

a) In the UK
b) Learner drivers/young drivers
c) A new written test consisting of 30 multiple-choice
   questions will have to be taken by all learner drivers
   before they take their driving test.
d) It will be introduced next July.
e) Because the majority of people taking their driving
   tests are aged between 17 and 25, and this is the age
   group responsible for 25 per cent of all road deaths
   and 20 per cent of all accidents. It is felt that they
   need to become more aware of safety on the roads.
f) The AA don't think the new test goes far enough.

Review 4 Exercise 5

a) X Name cards must be treated with respect.
b) ✔
c) X Giving business contacts a present on their
      birthday is unusual in Britain.
d) ✔
e) X The earthquake has made thousands of people
      homeless.
f) ✔
g) ✔
h) X By the end of last week we had seen no
      improvement in her health.
i) ✔
j) X Next year I think there will be a different party in
      government.
k) ✔
l) X We will see more people working from home in the
      next decade.
m) ✔
n) X By the end of next year 50 members of staff will
      have been sacked.
o) X I hoped that I would be invited to the party.
p) X I was afraid of becoming sick.
q) X What will you be doing this time next year?
r) ✔
s) ✔
t) ✔

TAPESCRIPTS

Unit 1 Exercise 3

1 Yes, it's funny in my country, Nigeria, in the south-west you mustn't ask how many children someone has, as this casts a spell. Counting children is wrong, as you can have as many children as you like.
2 If you come to Bangladesh, people will want to know all kinds of personal details – not just the names of your children but also their exact ages down to days and hours – but not minutes!
3 Vietnamese are very polite people and we don't like a lot of eye contact. It is also rude to ask if someone is married.
4 In some parts of Nigeria you can enquire about a person's salary. People are quite proud of how much they earn.
5 Actually in Korea we often ask how old someone is because their age affects the way in which we speak to them.

Unit 1 Exercise 4(c)

I think I'd stick to quite neutral topics like the weather and the flight. Family and personal life can be a bit difficult. I'd avoid them. I don't know about names, some people ask and others don't – I never ask someone's name. Borrowing a magazine or newspaper is OK, of course, and so is talking about the food and the journey. Asking the time is all right as well, but never, ever ask anyone about money – 'How much do you earn?' or 'How much did your coat cost?'. And nothing about age, like 'How old are you?'. Some people can get very upset if you do. Ask about the news and current affairs, by all means, but stay away from politics and, of course, religion!

Unit 2 Exercise 3(a)

Juan: For me writing isn't important because I don't need to write. Reading is important but I can improve my reading by myself. But to communicate, to speak, it's important to be at school with the teacher, to understand and to speak with good pronunciation and grammar.
Angela: Pronunciation is important. You can know a lot of words but if you don't have the correct pronunciation it's no good. Nobody understands you. And grammar too. If you want to speak correctly you have to know the form . . . you have to know all these things to speak correctly.
Yuko: Vocabulary – I have to think a lot about what I want to say and describe. I need to have more vocabulary. I can study for myself – but for me this is what's most important: help to learn vocabulary. I need vocabulary to speak. If I don't have it I can't speak.
Hiromi: My main problem is fluency and accuracy of speaking. The problem is spoken English. I feel more confident in my written English. You have time to think.
Sven: At work I have to translate letters so I need to write well – it's difficult. Reading and writing are the most important for me. I don't have to speak – not even on the telephone.
Jacek: Listening isn't easy. I can understand when it's written but when I watch TV or listen to music it's hard. I want to work on my listening and speaking.
Yves: Ten years ago I was able to speak English but I didn't pay enough attention to learning, to improving, or at least to not forgetting my English and when I came to England I realised that I had made a big mistake . . . I couldn't speak. For the future I hope to continue to study and review my studies so that I will keep up my English.

Unit 3 Exercise 1(a)

1 My first years were in the city of Oslo, well not quite downtown, but not out in the suburbs either. It was in a flat, it was on the first floor, a first floor flat, and I remember that we didn't have any wash-basins actually: we had to carry up our water. It was quite old-fashioned at that time and there we were not allowed to play. When we kept going on you went into the back yard either so we had to play, you know, on the streets.
2 The house I was born in was a single-storey house. When you came into it you came into a corridor where my parents used to keep meat because it was rather cold outside. When you kept going on you went into the dining room and there was a big stove in it where my mother used to cook food and we used to sit together next to it.
3 It was an apartment on the fifth floor in a town in Italy and I liked it very much because from certain windows I could see the sea and very beautiful sunsets, and from the other there was a park where children went to play. I didn't go usually because I was an only child so my parents used to keep me at home, but I liked to look at it through the windows and watch what was happening.
4 I've got vague memories of the house in which I lived between two and seven. It was near a small town near Madrid and I remember I was . . . it was a bungalow, just one floor, it had a porch, a big porch at the front door, and . . . behind the house there were fruit trees.
5 Well, it was quite a big flat in Paris and what I remember is that it had lots of bedrooms and when my sister and I walked along the corridor we used to look into the bedrooms and one of them was a dark bedroom with no windows And we used to get frightened passing it.
6 Well, it was a very big house in a little town in Austria and I remember very cold winters when I used to sit near the stove with my cat.
7 The house I used to live in was a semi-detached house in a little town in Spain and the most . . . the bedroom I remember most was the bedroom where my sisters and I used to play and to share our toys.

Unit 4 Exercise 1(c)

Interviewer: What are you going to do after you leave school?
Martin: Well, that'll be after the exams . . . and after I've spent months revising and then doing the exams – I expect I'll want a bit of a rest . . . a bit of a break. A whole group of us are going to have a holiday together, probably in Malta, just to chill out and let the world go by, you know, just for fun. Then in the autumn I'm going to live in Italy for three months, I think, and learn the language – I've got family there. Then . . . I don't know exactly. I'm going to have to get a job because I want to go to Africa with three of my mates but I don't know what kind of job. Hopefully I'll find something awful that's well paid, like night work in a factory or something . . .
Interviewer: And what are you going to do in Africa? Is it voluntary work, or teaching, things like that?
Martin: Not really, we're just going to travel around, backpacking, you know. We're going to go to Zimbabwe first, although we'll probably have to travel via South Africa because you can get really cheap flights to Johannesburg, and then travel around, Victoria Falls, that kind of thing. I'm not really sure . . . I've got this friend who did it last year, and she said Zanzibar was great, so I think we'll probably go through Mozambique to Malawi, which sounds great, and then go up to Tanzania and across to Zanzibar by boat.
Interviewer: It sounds as if you're going to need a lot of money.

Martin: Well, you can get really cheap flights to Jo'burg if you don't mind what airline you use, or where you stop or when you go. And then we'll camp – I'm going to buy a light tent, and we'll live cheaply. We're going to have to live on five pounds a day or so and I reckon we'll do a lot of walking.
Interviewer: And how long will you be away for?
Martin: Hopefully about four months – and then I'm going to start university . . . that's if I come back, that is!

Review 1 Exercise 2

Interviewer: Atsuko, why are you taking this course?
Atsuko: Well, you know my father thought it was a good idea.
Interviewer: Your father? Why?
Atsuko: He thinks that it is important for Japanese women to be well educated – to get a better husband!
Interviewer: Oh, I see. Is that the real reason you're doing this course, though?
Atsuko: No, no. I'm doing it for me, too. I need to improve my English. It's not so good.
Interviewer: Why do you need to improve it? It sounds OK to me.
Atsuko: Oh, no, no! Very kind, but it's not good enough for my job.
Interviewer: Tell me about your job, then.
Atsuko: My job? You want me to say about my job? OK. I work in export department of Panasonic. I need to write letters, faxes and all things like that.
Interviewer: I see. What about speaking English?
Atsuko: Oh yes, very much. Yes. I get phone calls from all over the world. Sometimes it's very hard to discuss on the phone. Sometimes the other people don't speak good English!
Interviewer: Right! What sort of things do you discuss on the phone?
Atsuko: Discuss? You mean me? Oh, well . . . I have to say about the products, you know? I have to say what they do, what new things there are. Sometimes also explain how things work. It's hard, you know!
Interviewer: Yes. What products do you have to talk about?
Atsuko: Products? You mean Panasonic products?
Interviewer: Er . . . yes, yes.
Atsuko: Oh um . . . telephone answering machines, for example. Sometimes also fax machine. Many different things. I have to know a lot of things in Japanese and English.
Interviewer: Yes, it sounds quite a challenge.
Atsuko: Challenge? Oh yes, yes.
Interviewer: Do you need English for other things as well?
Atsuko: Other things? You mean not for work?
Interviewer: Yes.
Atsuko: Oh yes. For my holidays. I like America, Australia and Europe. You have to know English to travel.
Interviewer: Right! Do you have any English-speaking friends?
Atsuko: Oh! Oh . . . only my boyfriend. He's English.
Interviewer: Is he? Does he speak Japanese?
Atsuko: No, no. Not really. We have to speak English all the time.
Interviewer: So, you need English for your social life, too.
Atsuko: Yes.
Interviewer: Is your father happy about you having a foreign boyfriend?
Atsuko: My father? Oh, no, no, no. He doesn't know! No!

Unit 5 Exercise 3(b)

Presenter: And now on *Family Life*, the programme which deals with the real issues of the family, we turn to the tricky question of divorce. In this week's discussion: 'Divorce and You'. Not divorce as it affects adults so much, but as it affects children. We have with us in the studio Angela French from Relation, the organisation which helps children in divorce situations. Angela, imagine I'm a child in the middle of a divorce: what kind of advice do you have for me?

Angela: Let's start with your feelings. You may be confused, angry, frightened or relieved about some things and sad about others. You may also find that these feelings seem to go on and on and make you behave in ways you don't normally. Things usually fall into place, and with time you'll feel normal again. If you're so upset that it's affecting your school work, friendship or hobbies, it's best to tell someone if you think it'll help. People can only help if you let them know what's happening.

Presenter: So tell someone . . .

Angela: Yes, talking about what worries you can help, though you may find your parents too upset or angry with each other to sit down and discuss it with you. So you need to look at other ways of getting help. If this is the case in your family, have a think about other adults you know who you can trust – another relative, a teacher, or a doctor perhaps. Adults don't always find it easy to start talking about important things like this, but if you ask them questions and let them know you need to talk, they will usually try to help.

Presenter: Yes . . .

Angela: As far as your parents go, they may have split up from each other but they're still your mum and dad. You may be worried that it will upset the parent you live with if you see your other parent, but it's OK for you to want to keep in touch with them both.

Presenter: And if they're living with someone else . . . ?

Angela: It's possible that one – or both – of your parents may find a new partner. You may feel angry, jealous, pushed out and thoroughly confused. Your feelings are important and reactions like this are quite understandable. If your parent's new partner has children, getting to know them, and perhaps having to live with them, will certainly be difficult to begin with. But you may find that in time you become close friends. Remember, they'll be finding it difficult too.

Unit 7 Exercise 2(b)

I don't get on with my parents, like. In fact, I, you know, I hate them. They criticise everything I do. Everything. They won't let me be me, you know. Yeah, then they nag nag nag me all the time. 'You must do better at school, Kevin', 'This is no good, Kevin'. Well, I hate school, don't I? It's boring and my teachers are all bloody stupid, you know? Yeah, and always getting at me and all. Like, my parents, yeah?, want me to get qualifications, right, but what for? You know? There ain't any jobs, are there? Look, I just want to do what I want to do, yeah? Get a motorbike, a good bike, yeah, travel about, see the world. Know what I mean? I tell you, they don't like my friends and . . . like, they won't let them in the house. Bloody hell! I'm not allowed to stay out later than 10 pm in the week, like. Yeah. Huh! You know what else? My dad's stopped my pocket money, right, so I can't go down the pub with my mates. Like, he goes on at me all the time – he says everything I do is rubbish, everything. You know what? Sometimes I get angry, like, very angry, like I want to . . . kill him, smash his head in, you know? Last week, my mates and me got some spray paint. Yeah. That was cool. We went bananas. Oh yeah! We sprayed stuff all over the shopping centre walls, shops and that, yeah, all over 'em, at night, like, Pillheads Rule! Pillheads Rule! Yay! Pillheads is the name of our gang, like. But my parents just don't understand . . .

Unit 7 Exercise 4

Conversation 1

A: I tell you, I'm going bananas! It's really getting to me!

B: Why? What's the matter?

A: Well, he just comes home every night after work at about 7 o'clock and thinks that's it for the day.

B: You mean, he puts his feet up?

A: Huh! Do I! He just flops on the sofa with a glass of whisky and reads the paper. The only thing he says is, 'What's for dinner tonight?' and 'Did you pick up my dry-cleaning?'. He doesn't ask me about my day. He

doesn't offer to help with the dinner. He hates it if the kids are noisy.

B: Have you tried telling him that you're upset?

A: Yes, but he doesn't want to talk about it. What on earth can I do?

Conversation 2

C: That's better . . . Oh I needed that. Boy, do I need that . . .

D: What's up with you, then?

C: Nothing.

D: Right.

C: Ah well, all right. I need your advice on something.

D: What's that, then? Trouble with the car again?

C: What? Oh no, it's . . . it's . . . Yvette.

D: Oh? I thought you two were fine.

C: Hmm, well, we're not. She's always going on at me about working late.

D: Yeah, well you can't help that. You need to work late if you want to get on.

C: I know, I know, but she's so jealous! She thinks I'm trying to get off with Dorothy, my secretary.

D: Are you?

C: Wouldn't mind . . . but no, no I wouldn't do that. Yvette's just crazy. She won't even let me go to my evening class in computer programming. She just doesn't trust me.

D: Oh, what a pain in the bum.

C: Yeah, too right, mate. What's your advice?

Conversation 3

E: You're like a brother to me, you know.

F: And you're like a brother to me, too, old friend. But you look a bit troubled. Is there something wrong?

E: Well, I don't know how to put it, really. It's very awkward, you know.

F: What is?

E: Well, I want to ask you what I should do about Peter.

F: What about him?

E: Ah! Yesterday he came to my home, and . . . and he kissed my mother!

F: Er . . . yes?

E: But he should not!

F: No . . . er . . . how do you mean, he kissed your mother?

E: I introduced him to my mother and he just went, 'Hello, Mrs Mahmoud' and kiss, kiss on both sides of her face! He kissed my mother!

F: What did she do?

E: My mother screamed and pushed him off and he fell on the floor.

F: Ha ha ha!

E: No, it's not funny. In my culture you can only kiss the woman who is your wife.

F: Sorry. Yes, I know. Oh dear. They got off on the wrong foot, didn't they? What happened afterwards?

E: I had to throw him out because my mother was so angry. So now he's angry with me. He won't talk to me. My mother won't get over it. I don't know what to do. What would you do?

Unit 8 Exercise 2

First caller

Presenter: And now let's go to line 2. Is that Derek?

Derek: Yes, that's right.

Presenter: And what's your true confession, Derek?

Derek: It's something I did when I was 19 and I've always felt a bit bad about it.

Presenter: OK, Derek, let's hear all about it.

Derek: When I was living in Manchester, I worked in an office with a group of other young blokes. Next to the office was a big supermarket and we used to hang around there at lunchtimes. It was quite boring so we were always looking for ways to liven things up. One day we decided to play a small, harmless practical joke.

Presenter: Uh-huh.

Derek: Well, it was a Wednesday lunchtime. Me and my three friends, Neil, Peter, and Richard, were standing by the supermarket entrance. We were well prepared. Neil was holding a big watch, Peter had a large envelope with the supermarket's name on it, and Richard and I were carrying two bunches of flowers for our lucky winner.

Presenter: Winner? Winner of what?

Derek: Wait and see. We stood by the doorway and waited for the next customer. Then she came in. It was an old lady of about seventy. At once we all stepped

forward. Richard and I gave her the flowers and Peter shouted: 'Congratulations! You are the millionth customer this year! You've won a free three-minute trolley push. Push the trolley around the supermarket for three minutes and take as many things as you want – free! Take as much as you can for three minutes and take it home, free!'

Presenter: Really?

Derek: The old lady gave a huge smile and a shout and grabbed the nearest trolley. She ran as fast as she could and filled the trolley with food. She started with the tins, and next she moved to the meat. After that, the vegetables. It was a marvellous sight.

Presenter: I can just imagine. Do go on.

Derek: Well, that old lady had the energy and enthusiasm of a twenty-year-old. In two minutes she'd finished the whole food section. And then, with the trolley almost full of food, she headed for the wine department. At that moment we decided to leave and ran out of the supermarket.

Presenter: So how did it end?

Derek: Well, like this. I . . . don't want to apologise to the old lady, who I feel really enjoyed her trip around the supermarket. However, I would like to apologise to the manager who tried to stop a very strong and lively lady as she ran from the supermarket with a trolley full of stolen goods. The manager was standing in the supermarket doorway when the trolley hit him on the knee, breaking it in two places. He was taken to hospital, and the old lady escaped with the trolley full of food.

Second caller

Presenter: And now our last caller of the morning. Kathy on line 3. Good morning Kathy.

Kathy: Good morning. I'm ringing from Scotland, but this is about when I was living in London.

Presenter: Lovely. So let's hear what happened.

Kathy: This was when I was 19 and I had met my dream man. His name was Ralph and he worked for a sports equipment company. We were engaged to be married. I had never known anyone like him. He was tall and dark with a beautiful body. He often had to travel abroad and I went with him. So I had lots of weekends in Paris, the odd week in Spain and Italy and even three weeks in Sydney, Australia.

Presenter: I see.

Kathy: Well, he had arranged a trip to America. He was going for five months, travelling around, buying sports equipment for his company. I wanted to give up my job and go with him. But Ralph persuaded me to stay in London. He told me I'd done so well in my job it would be a shame to lose it. Anyway, he said there was no point in my coming with him, as he'd be too busy to spend time with me. I was young and believed everything he said. So I stayed in London and Ralph went to America.

Presenter: Yes . . . ?

Kathy: Then a friend of mine who had driven Ralph to the airport told me that Ralph had taken another woman with him to the USA. He had lied to me and had taken someone else! I got so angry. I was even more angry because Ralph was away and I couldn't do anything to him. His house was locked up and I didn't have a key so I couldn't go around and smash it up or anything. Then I remembered that Mr Superman Ralph had one thing he was afraid of: mice! So I immediately went around to the pet shop and bought four mice, two male and two female. And then I went round to Ralph's house and put the mice through the letter-box in the front door. Every night I came around to the house and put food for the mice through the letter box.

Presenter: What happened next?

Kathy: I fed the mice every day. In the end, Ralph was away for seven months and sent me a 'I've met someone else' letter. Finally, the great day came when he returned home. The same friend went to collect Ralph and his new girlfriend and took them to the house. Ralph unlocked the door and stepped in with his arm around his new lady. She screamed! Ralph screamed! There were mice everywhere. Hundreds of mice! they had eaten the carpets and the furniture. They had dug holes in the floors and had damaged everything. Ralph was too frightened to go into the house. His new girlfriend left him. In the end, Ralph managed to get someone to come around and kill the mice. But he had to sell his house because of the memory of them. And the only ones I felt sorry for are the mice!

Review 2 Exercise 2

Interviewer: Welcome back after that break. This is Anna James and *Talking Points*, and today we're asking, 'Should parents be allowed to divorce?'. Before the break we heard from a number of parents who have divorced and all of them felt that it had been the right thing to do. Generally speaking, the parents felt it was better to divorce than to bring children up in a marriage which was at best loveless and, at its worst, full of antagonism and bad feeling. But how do the children feel? Let's find out.

Louise is 15. Her parents divorced when she was four, but have remained friends. Louise's father picks her up and takes her to school almost every morning. He has her to stay two nights a week and alternate weekends, and the family has Sunday lunch together. Theirs is a . . . what we might call 'a perfect divorce'. Is it perfect, Louise? How do you feel about it?
Louise: Well, my parents have given me lots of love and attention, so I can't complain. But when your parents are divorced, you can't be a child like someone in a proper family can. I feel like I have to be a friend and a companion and sometimes a support for my parents.
Interviewer: Do you feel you missed out on your childhood, then?
Louise: In a way, yes. I feel I had to be grown up about things too soon.
Interviewer: Do you wish your parents were still together?
Louise: Oh yes. Even now. I wish so much that we could all be together. It's been confusing because my parents get on so well and there's never been any unpleasantness between them. Once I suggested we get a big house and divide it so they could have their separate parts, but they say they can't live under the same roof.
Interviewer: Are you disappointed by that?
Louise: Yeah, yeah, I am. You know, if I, if I see a film about happy families or read about one in a book it hurts. But worst of all is seeing families on holiday and having fun and laughing together and all that. I just want to cry or scream.
Interviewer: Mmm. So, even when it's a good divorce, it can still hurt the children, it seems. What's it like for children whose parents argue and fight? Let's talk to Charlie. He's 17 now. His parents divorced when he was five. What are your memories, Charlie, and have they affected you, do you think?
Charlie: Yeah, yeah, they have, I'd say. My parents married when they were very young and um . . . they weren't really suited. I've vivid memories of them putting each other down, even though I was very small. There were huge rows, like – like thunderstorms. They filled the house. It was really frightening. If, if they were shut in a room, I used to stand outside, listening and, and wondering what it all meant. Yeah. Last year, me and my sister moved out and we share a flat now with some friends. We don't see much of mum and dad. It's better to be away from home now.
Interviewer: It seems as if children of divorced parents might well disagree with the view that the parents have on divorce. Suzanne is 16. Her parents divorced when she was 14 and she lives with her mother and two younger brothers. She sees her father once or twice a week. Suzanne, what's your opinion of divorce?
Suzanne: Well, I know there's no easy answer, is there? I've decided, though, if, if I marry and have children, I'm determined I'll make it work. I wouldn't want them to feel like I do. I . . . I think parents can make more effort if they really decide to, but sometimes they're more like children than we are.
Interviewer: Well, what is the answer? Should parents be allowed to divorce? Is a sham marriage better than no marriage as far as the children are concerned? Whose feelings are more important – the children's or the parents'? If you have a view, please call our phone line now. The number is . . .

Unit 9 Exercise 2(a)

Yale: Oh! Oh, God. Boy, I really feel good, you know. I've got my life together finally.
Ike: Yeah?

Yale: Yeah, you know I just had to cut this thing off finally. I'm not the type for affairs. You know, I finally figured it out.
Ike: Do you – do you ever hear from Mary or see her or anything?
Yale: No, no we just – you know, cut it off. I think it's easier that way, you know?
Ike: Ah-ha.
Yale: She's a terrific person. She deserves more than a fling with a married guy.
Ike: Yeah, she's great. She's a little screwed up but great.
Yale: Yeah, well, that's right up your alley, you know. I think you ought to call her.
Ike: I – I should call her?
Yale: Yeah.
Ike: Why should I call her?
Yale: Because she likes you. She told me she did.
Ike: You're crazy.
Yale: No, I'm not. She said she finds you attractive.
Ike: She – she said she found me attractive?
Yale: Yeah.
Ike: Yeah, when was this?
Yale: Oh, she said it when she first met you.
Ike: I didn't know. I can't.
Yale: Sorry about that.
Ike: I can't. I think – I always think of you two guys as together. I – I don't think that I could.
Yale: No. It's over, it's over. Unless you're serious about Tracy. Are you serious about Tracy?
Ike: No, Tracy's too young.
Yale: Well, then call her up. Listen, she's an unhappy person, you know. I mean she – she needs something in her life. I mean, I think you guys would be good together.

Unit 9 Exercise 2(b)

Ike: Hey.
Mary: What?
Ike: Come here.
Mary: What? What're you doing?
Ike: What am I doing? You have to ask what I'm doing? I was kissing you flush on the mouth.
Mary: Oh, Jesus, I don't know. I – I – boy, I cannot get my life in any kind of order. It's just . . .
Ike: Well, it's something I wanted to do for the longest time, you know, and . . . and . . .
Mary: Yeah, yeah, I know.
Ike: Do you?
Mary: Uh-huh.
Ike: 'Cause I – I – I thought I was hiding it. I was trying to be real cool and casual.
Mary: Oh, I thought you wanted to kiss me that day at the planetarium.
Ike: Yeah, I did.
Mary: Yeah, I thought so.
Ike: But . . . but you were – you were – going out with Yale then . . .
Mary: Hm-hm.
Ike: And I would never in a million years, you know, interfere in anything like that. I just . . . well, did you want me to kiss you then? I mean . . .
Mary: Mm, I don't know what I wanted . . . I was so angry at Yale that day.

Unit 9 Exercise 2(c)

Mary: Before you get wound up, there's something I – I want to tell you.
Ike: What's the matter? You look – you look pale.
Mary: Well.
Ike: Well, wha – what's the matter? Hey, what – Is there something wrong? What is it?
Mary: I . . . think I'm still in love with Yale.
Ike: What? You – Are you kidd . . .? You are?
Mary: Yes.
Ike: Well, when did this happen? I mean, what . . .? Well, you are or you think you are?
Mary: I started seeing him again.
Ike: When? Since when?
Mary: Uh . . . just since today. We're not really . . . That's why I wanted to be open about it.
Ike: Jesus, I'm . . . I'm shocked. I'm – I'm . . . shocked. I'm . . . surprised.

Unit 10 Exercise 3(a)

Presenter: Good evening and welcome to *Issues for Today*. Our topic tonight is experiments on animals and to start the discussion we have a strongly argued appeal from Jeff Sachs of the animal rights organisation Animal Aid. Now, Jeff, what's all the fuss about? After all, 85 per cent of doctors support experiments on animals.
Jeff Sachs: This is first and foremost a moral question. What kind of people are we? As humans, we live in a society which protects the rights of the weak. We take care of the sick, the old and the disabled and punish those who are violent to others. But we also have a darker, cruel side. I believe that we experiment on animals because they are powerless to stop us, and we count their pain as unimportant when measured against our own interests. We live unhealthy lives and make animals suffer in the search for cures for our illnesses. We even see the production of a new lipstick as a good enough reason to inflict pain on animals.

It's not that we think animals can't feel pain – we know very well that they do. And it's dangerous to say that we use animals in experiments because they lack our intelligence. After all, this argument would allow us to experiment on mentally handicapped humans.

Animals have feelings. Like us, they can suffer pain, fear and mental agony. Like us, each has a life to live. A rat's life is important to a rat, whatever value a human may place on it. Why should one individual animal be made to suffer for the supposed benefit of people? Is it right to kill one human being in an experiment to save thousands of others? What if that human were you?
Presenter: Well, yeah, thank you, Jeff. Some strong stuff there.
Jeff Sachs: Yeah, well it's an important issue . . .
Presenter: Yeah, well thank you. Now – now let's hear the opposing point of view from Dr Clark of the Medical Research Group.
Dr Clark: Yeah – strong stuff indeed, and quite dangerous too. Let's get things straight. First of all, most of us eat animals. Is Jeff arguing that we must all become vegetarians and stop eating meat? Secondly, and most importantly, over the last 100 years medical research has produced many ways to treat and prevent diseases such as polio and save lives through operations like heart transplants. None of this was possible without animal research. Does Jeff want humans to die to save the lives of animals? Thirdly, and this is an interesting question, is Jeff against animal research to find cures for sick animals? If he isn't, why is it wrong to do the same experiments to find cures for sick people?
Presenter: Dr Clark, thank you. Well now, you've heard the arguments. Now let's hear what you, the audience, and you at home think . . .

Unit 11 Exercise 1(c)

. . . somebody who's accurate, is fast, who's got an open mind, who's not prejudiced in any way, who can see both sides of a story, ask for both sides of a story, has humour, can be serious, can talk to people and get people to talk back . . .

Unit 11 Exercise 2(c)

A: I expect you have to use English sometimes at work.
B: No, I don't really. But I had to two weeks ago when we had a visit from two representatives from Bristol. Then I had to speak English. And every time when I meet an Englishman I become very nervous because I haven't been practise English . . . practising English for several years . . . for many years, so I become really nervous because I'm afraid of saying something wrong. Then when I meet people from other countries and use the English language, I think I can manage rather well . . . because they can't speak English themselves . . . often they can't . . .
A: So there's a difference . . .
B: It's a difference, yes.
A: What happened when you had the visit from England?
B: Oh, well, we talked a lot during a coffee break, just that . . .
A: And what did you talk about?

B: Oh we talked about several things. We were many people, you know, so I didn't have to speak all the time. It's much easier to speak English when you are ... when there are several people present because you can get time to find the right words and you aren't stressed to find the right words. You get time and that's important, I think. But if you sit like I am doing just now, you have to find the words immediately and then you get nervous.
A: How have you found using English as a tourist when you've travelled abroad?
B: It doesn't bother me ...
A: Why?
B: When I'm in Spain it's much easier to speak English because they can't speak English as natives. It's much easier for me and I can order anything in a restaurant, for example, and I can speak of anything in a shop and so ... it's always difficult ... but if you get a whisky or two it's much easier, yes ...

Unit 12 Exercise 1

A: Yes, can we help you?
B: Do you want us to do something? Now? No. Later? No.
C: Tomorrow? Yes. At what time?
A: At four. In the afternoon?
B: In the morning. You want breakfast at four? No. Sleep? Wake up? Do you want us to wake you at four?
C: Yes. You're going to leave the hotel. No. You're not leaving.
A: You're going to go somewhere. Is it for business? No. For pleasure? Yes.
B: You're doing exercises. You're moving your arms.
A: You're going skiing. You want us to wake you at four tomorrow morning because you're going skiing.
Participant: Yes. That's right!

Unit 12 Exercise 2(c)

1 Rub your hands together.
2 Support your head with your hands.
3 Touch your nose.
4 Cover your right eye.
5 Rest your left hand on your knee.
6 Stroke your left arm.
7 Scratch your right arm.

Review 3 Exercise 1

Interviewer: You experienced a misunderstanding when you worked in Singapore, didn't you?
Carol: Mmm, yes – quite a few, actually.
Interviewer: Tell us about one, then.
Carol: Um, well ... let me see ... oh yes, I know.
Interviewer: Yes?
Carol: Well, I had this red lump on my left leg. Just above the knee. Sort of like a mole, you know? Anyway, I had it for years and it never bothered me much.
Interviewer: Mm-hm.
Carol: Well, after I'd been in Singapore for a while, I noticed that I had a sort of pain in my left leg. I can't really describe it. It sort of felt like pressure, you know, like something was pressing on a nerve. Drove me mad. I couldn't sleep. It seemed to be just in the area where this red lump was. So then I started to get worried.
Interviewer: Mmm.
Carol: You know how it is in the middle of the night when you can't sleep and you start to imagine all sorts of things. I imagined the doctor telling me I had cancer and that I'd have to have my leg cut off. I imagined what my life would be like with only one leg – and how brave and noble I'd be, well, you know how it is. Next morning, I'd go to work and forget about it again.
Interviewer: Mmm.
Carol: One night, though, the pain was really bad and I got so scared. Next day I went to the doctor's.
Interviewer: What did he say?
Carol: Well, in Singapore, doctors aren't reassuring like they are at home. You know, at home they tell you it's nothing, not to worry – in Singapore it's the opposite; they always seem to think the worst and they let you know, too. 'Oh', he said, 'it looks serious. You'd better have it removed immediately.' Oh, I felt terrified. My worst nightmare!
Interviewer: Yeah!

Carol: Anyway, I went along to the hospital and they cut out the lump and stitched me up. The doctor showed me the lump – oh, it was horrible! It was much bigger than I'd realised. I heard him say to his assistant, 'Oh, that's a big one. Get it to the lab for tests right away.' I was told to return in five days to have my stitches out and get my result. Of course, I felt really shaky by the time they'd finished. A bit in shock, I suppose. I wandered out and made an appointment at the reception desk for five days later and left. I tried not to think about it while I waited. On the day I was to go back to the hospital I got out my appointment card to check what time I had to be there and, oh my God, I'd missed it! It was the day before! I really panicked. I phoned up the hospital and they told me any doctor could remove my stitches, so that wasn't a problem. Then I asked if I could have my results.
Interviewer: Go on ...
Carol: The receptionist said that the doctor wasn't in, but she'd put me through to his assistant. Oh, my heart was pounding by this time and my mouth was all dry.
Interviewer: With the stress?
Carol: You bet. I was really nervous. Anyhow, the assistant said, 'OK' and told me 'Hold on' while she got my card. When she got back to the phone she said, 'I think you'd better come in and talk to the doctor in person.' Oh, I was so shocked.
Interviewer: Oh dear!
Carol: 'Why?' I asked. 'Is there something wrong?' Pause ... 'Well,' she said, 'it's best if the doctor tells you himself, then he can explain it properly and tell you about the treatment.' So ... there's me thinking, 'Oh my God, this is it. I've got cancer. I felt literally sick. I tried to make an appointment, but the doctor's list was full up and, to make things worse, he was going on holiday for two weeks the next day! 'So when can I talk to him?' I asked. His assistant said she'd get him to call me when he got in later that morning.
Interviewer: Oh no, poor you! What did you do?
Carol: Oh, I went to work. But I couldn't concentrate or think straight. Every time the phone rang, I nearly passed out. I kept ringing the hospital, but the doctor was late. Eventually, he rang me. Oh, I was really shaking. He said, 'Ms Smith?' I said, 'Yes?' 'Oh, everything's fine,' he said. 'No further treatment necessary.' What? I made him say it three times, I said, 'So why didn't your assistant tell me that? It would have saved me all this worry!' 'I don't know,' he said. He did apologise, though.
Interviewer: How scary!
Carol: Yeah. A couple of days later I got a letter from the hospital with the results of the tests. On it it said that I'd had some kind of 'tumour'. I looked it up in a medical dictionary and it explained that it was a benign kind of tumour. I think the assistant must have seen the word 'tumour' and immediately thought it meant cancer. That was a day I'll never forget.
Interviewer: So, there were two misunderstandings ...
Carol: Er, yes ... first of all, I didn't realise there was a cultural difference and that all doctors say everything is serious because they're expected to. It makes them more important. So that made me scared right from the start. At home, if a doctor says it's serious, then it's very very serious!
Interviewer: Yes.
Carol: Yeah, and the other misunderstanding was the assistant not realising it wasn't a cancerous tumour. She probably thought she was being very kind and sensitive!

Unit 13 Exercise 2(a)

Two men meet on a plane from Tokyo to Hong Kong. Chu Hon-fai is a Hong Kong exporter who is returning from a business trip to Japan. Andrew Richardson is an American buyer on his first business trip to Hong Kong. It's a convenient meeting for them because Mr Chu's company sells some of the products Mr Richardson has come to Hong Kong to buy. After a bit of conversation, they introduce themselves to each other.

Unit 13 Exercise 2(b)

Mr Richardson: By the way, I'm Andrew Richardson. My friends call me Andy. This is my business card.
Mr Chu: I'm Mr Chu. Pleased to meet you Mr Richardson. This is my card.

Mr Richardson: No, no. Call me Andy. I think we'll be doing a lot of business together.
Mr Chu: Yes, I hope so.
Mr Richardson: 'Chu, Hon-fai'. Hon-fai, I'll give you a call tomorrow as soon as I get settled at my hotel.
Mr Chu: Yes, I'll expect your call.

Unit 13 Exercise 2(c)

Mr Richardson: I'm really pleased to have met Mr Chu and I think we've gotten off to a good start. We're using our first names and Mr Chu's smile shows that he's friendly and easy to do business with. I really look forward to meeting him again.
Mr Chu: I'm afraid I feel quite uncomfortable with Mr Richardson. I think he will be difficult to work with. He doesn't seem to understand cultural differences. I smiled when he used my first name because I was embarrassed – no one calls me by that name. I prefer to use 'Mr'. I'm worried about meeting Mr Richardson again.

Unit 13 Exercise 4(a)

Years ago I spent a year at a Swedish university as an exchange student. One day my professor invited me to her house. She was having a summer party. Just a few friends around the swimming pool, five o'clock on Saturday.

Well, I knew two things about parties in Sweden: first of all, you must be on time, and secondly, you must bring something with you, some sort of present. So I bought a nice big bunch of flowers and caught an early bus on Saturday afternoon. I was wearing a very smart new yellow shirt and a pair of bright red shorts.

But ... it was pretty warm and the bus was crowded, and I fell asleep ... so I missed my stop. When I woke up, the bus was almost empty. So I jumped off at the next stop and started to run back to the professor's place. And then I realised I'd left the flowers on the bus! It was no use. The bus had gone. I arrived half an hour late, sweating ... red shorts, red face and no present. I looked around at the other guests and they were all wearing formal clothes – suits and party dresses. I felt awful.

Anyway, I found the professor and apologised. And then it was time to meet people. In Sweden when you arrive at a party you have to go around and shake hands with everyone there. As you shake hands you say your name and nod your head slightly, and then you move on to the next person. There's no conversation – it's impossible, because new arrivals keep coming and introducing themselves.

Well, after that we played games on the grass: darts and mini-golf and a kind of tennis game. The professor said there was a special prize for the winner. So everyone concentrated and again, there was no conversation. So different from parties in England, where all people do is talk. Everything seemed so cold and formal to me.

Finally we sat down to dinner at tables round the pool. Food was brought out and there was wine – lots of bottles were opened. I knew what was coming next: toasts. In Sweden you don't drink when you want to, you all drink together at the same time. The host raises a glass, you do the same and look everyone on your table in the eye. Then you empty your glass and look everyone in the eye again before putting down the glass. We did this lots of times! And the atmosphere changed completely. People started laughing and talking. Someone started singing and everyone joined in. And more wine was poured ...

And then the professor stood up to announce the winner of the games we'd played. I couldn't believe my ears. I was the winner. I looked around and smiled. The professor smiled too, and said that the prize was to be the first person to go swimming. Oh no! The other people at my table grabbed me and dragged me over to the pool. I tried to get away, but they picked me up and threw me in with all my clothes on – red shorts and all! There was a great splash. Everyone laughed. Then there was another splash, and another one. Two of the guests had jumped into the pool – they were fully dressed too, in their party gear. And then everyone put on swimming things and joined in.

After swimming, there was hot coffee and more singing and dancing. It was a great party. But different from what I'd expected.

Unit 14 Exercise 2(a)

Good evening and welcome to *Not the News*. Top stories tonight include an unusual way of guarding jewellery, the world's most married woman, a 'lost' Picasso, and the golfer with the most holes in one. And now here's the news in detail.

A large store in Holland has come up with an original way of looking after its window display of jewellery worth 2.7 million dollars. For the next four weeks the jewels are being guarded by four killers. The store has hired four deadly rattlesnakes to do the job. The snakes lie in the window with the jewels in full view of the public. So far, nothing has been stolen!

Linda Essex, the world's most married woman, is at it again. Linda, who has been married and divorced more times than any other woman, plans to marry in London again today. Linda has so far married 15 different men, five of them twice, and one of them three times. The longest marriage lasted seven years, the shortest 30 hours. Who knows, by the time you hear this she may be divorced again.

A 'lost' painting by Picasso was sold for a record sum of 3.2 million dollars at an auction in New York yesterday. The painting of a dog, which has been missing for over 30 years, was found by chance on the wall of a Brooklyn apartment. The painting, called *Chien Fou*, had been hanging in the kitchen since the owner, a Mrs Schultz, returned from a trip to Europe in the '60s. 'It's a nice picture,' she said, 'if you like dogs. Personally I prefer dollars.'

Golf Digest magazine reports that in California a golfer, Scott Palmer, has had 18 holes in one since 1983. To hit a golf ball so that it goes straight into the hole is almost impossible – the odds have been calculated at 33,000 to 1. Yet Palmer has done it 18 times – and the most amazing thing is that he has always used the same ball.

Unit 14 Exercise 5(b)

Good evening and welcome to *News 2010*, the world news report brought to you by CCN. First, the news from Britain.

The ex-Queen has been arrested. She was stopped last night at Heathrow Airport as she attempted to enter the country. The President of the British Republic, John Major, said that she had been refused permission to return to Britain. It is believed that the ex-Queen had been trying to visit her son, Charles, who has been in prison since the revolution last year. A government spokesperson said that the ex-Queen had been sent back to her new home in Russia on the next plane.

The weather continues hot and dry. It is now over a year since there has been any rain. Much of the country is now desert and camels have been imported from Egypt. A government spokesperson denied any connection between the lack of rain and the revolution, saying, 'If you can't stand the heat, go and join the Queen in Russia.'

And now the rest of the news. The cease-fire in Zurich broke down again last night as opposing forces attacked each other with artillery. Government troops attacked the town from three sides and five shells hit the Zurich Hotel, where most of the foreign refugees are staying, setting part of the hotel on fire. Local police said the shots were from a tank in a suburb still held by rebels. However, a United Nations peacekeeper from South Africa said the building had been hit by fire from government forces. There was no word on casualties and no sign of an end to the year-long civil war.

The drouble, the new world currency after the amalgamation of the dollar and the rouble last year, has been revalued against all other planetary currencies. It is ten cents higher against the Martian Bar, and twenty cents higher against Moon Money. This is a greater increase in value than had been predicted.

And that's the world news on 24th January 2010. Good-night.

Unit 15 Exercise 3

Oscar Denim was born in 1838 and died right at the end of the nineteenth century in 1899. He emigrated to New York in 1862 and spent the rest of his life in the American West, selling the hard-wearing blue cloth to which he gave his name. He soon became very wealthy and at his death gave a great deal of money to charity, including the foundation of the Denim Travelling Scholarships. These scholarships provided clothing and money to young Americans travelling to Europe.

William Henry Hoover was an American manufacturer who lived between 1849 and 1932. Around 1907 he developed the vacuum cleaner and soon all vacuum cleaners were known as Hoovers.

Noah Ketchup lived from 1680 to 1746 and was an American Indian. He was unsuccessful at a variety of occupations before moving to Philadelphia in 1700. There he began bottling and selling the excellent tomato sauce that his wife, Martha used to make. Everyone loved the sauce and soon the American Army made it standard issue with every meal. Ketchup, unfortunately, made little money from his invention.

Imre Kiosk (1862–1921) was born in Budapest, the son of an innkeeper and his wife. While still a young man, Kiosk made a large fortune from a chain of tiny shops selling tobacco, newspapers, soft drinks and sweets. Before the First World War there were 400 such shops all over Eastern Europe. The war ruined him and he died in poverty in Vienna.

John Montague, the fourth Earl of Sandwich, was a British politician who lived between 1718 and 1792. He was in charge of the British navy during the American Revolution but preferred gambling. He invented sandwiches, which are named after him, so that he could continue gambling without stopping to eat a meal.

Otis P. Walkman was an American inventor born in Greenwich, Connecticut. He is best known for the development of a device enabling the wearer to listen to music anywhere. Unfortunately the technology available at that time was so poor that the device had to be pulled behind the wearer on a small wheeled cart. It was many years before technological developments really made his invention both portable and popular.

Review 4 Exercise 1

It is important to realise that the Fijians' culture dictates that they should always invite a stranger into their home, whether they can afford to feed that stranger or not. Before the visit, if you have the opportunity, buy a kilo of *kava* root from an outdoor market. It is a traditional gift. Your host will gladly accept the gift and may perform a welcoming ritual that says your visit is officially recognised by the village. You will be offered a drink of *yaqona*, which, of course, you should accept and drink in one big gulp rather than in sips. When invited inside a *bure*, remove your shoes. Place them outside the door and stoop slightly when entering. Avoid standing fully upright indoors. It's bad manners. Dress modestly when visiting a village. Men should not be bare-chested and women should wear trousers or a long dress and definitely not shorts or a bathing suit. When entering a village, take off your hat.

ACKNOWLEDGEMENTS

The authors wish to thank the following people for their help in the production of this course:

Peter Donovan for his guidance, support and encouragement; our editors, James Dingle and Meredith Levy, for their professionalism, hard work, excellent editing skills and cheerful, supportive demeanour; Quinton Wong for their innovative design and great sense of humour; Anne Colwell for her design management; the illustrators for providing colour and chuckles.

All the people who have allowed us to use their photographs and names; all the people who gave their time to appear in photographs; James Richardson, the actors and all at Studio AVP for the recordings.

We would like to acknowledge ideas and inspiration from colleagues past and present, from learners and teachers on training courses, and from the many teachers whose classes we have been privileged to observe.

We have drawn stimulus from many sources and would like to acknowledge in particular *Drama Techniques in Language Learning* by Maley and Duff (Cambridge University Press), *Classroom Dynamics* by Hadfield (Oxford University Press), *Lessons from the Learner* by Deller (Addison Wesley Longman) and *The Red Book of Groups* by Houston (Rochester Foundation) to all of which the teacher is advised to turn for further support.

Reading material is taken from authentic sources and these are acknowledged. The material itself has in almost every case been adapted and abridged.

Listening material is based on transcripts of original recordings with some specially written material. We are very grateful to all those who permitted themselves to be recorded.

Learning to Learn English by Ellis and Sinclair (Cambridge University Press) is a key text and users of this book will recognise the source of our underlying philosophy.

This course is dedicated to Philip William James Sinclair.

The author and publishers would like to thank the following individuals and institutions for their help in writing reports, testing the material and for the invaluable feedback which they provided:

Susan Garvin, Bauffe, Belgium; Ricardo Sili da Silva, Cultura Inglesa, Rio de Janeiro, Brazil; Jirina Babáková, Mladá Boleslav, Czech Republic; LS-Kieliopisto, Tampere, Finland; Diann Gruber, Champs sur Marne, France; Metaform-Langues, Chamalières, France; International House Language School, Budapest, Hungary; Wall Street Institute, Milan, Italy; Centro Linguistico di Ateneo, Parma, Italy; Tom Hinton, British Council Cambridge English School, Kyoto, Japan; Crown Institute of Studies, Auckland, New Zealand; Barbara Duff, British Council, Muscat, Oman; LINK, Gliwice, Poland; International House, Coimbra, Portugal; ELCRA-Bell, Geneva, Switzerland; Volkshochschule, Zürich, Switzerland; International House, Bangkok, Thailand; Roger Scott, Bournemouth, UK; Cambridge Academy of English, Cambridge, UK; Tony Robinson, Eurocentres, Cambridge, UK; Eurocentres, London, UK; Hampstead Garden Suburb Institute, London, UK; Jeremy Jacobson, Truro, UK.

The authors and publishers are grateful to the authors, publishers and others who have given permission for the use of copyright material identified in the text. It has not been possible to identify the sources of all the material used and in such cases the publishers would welcome information from copyright owners.

Pricilla Ann Goslin for the excerpt on p. 7 from *Carioca Body Language*; EFL Services Ltd for quotes on p. 10; The Guardian for 'When I first visited England' on p. 16, the extract from *'We like it here'* by Leslie Plommer, the article on p. 25, text no. 1 on p. 46, the extract from *'S2bn Worldwide project leads torrent of breakthroughs'* by Tim Radford and the extract on pp. 49 and 50 from the video *'Making it'* by Shelton Fleming, © The Guardian; IPC Magazines for the questionnaire 'How long will you live?' on p. 20 from *Me Magazine* and the quotes on p. 68 from the *New Scientist supplement* of 15/10/94; Bee Murphy for the concept for the *Treasure* cartoons on pp. 24 and 25; Times Newspapers, 1995 for the article by Liz Jones on p. 22; The Observer for the article by Andrew Billen on p. 29, © The Observer; Solo Syndication Ltd for the article from The Daily Mail no. 2 on p. 46; The Independent for articles no. 3 by Susan Watts and no. 4 by Celia Hall on p. 46, © The Independent; The Telegraph for text no. 5 on p. 46, the extract from 'Human hearts bred in pigs for transplants' by David Fletcher, © The Telegraph plc, London, 1993; Sheldon Press for the text on p. 55 from *Body Language* by Allan Pease. Used by permission of the publishers; Management Books 2000 Ltd for the checklist on p. 56 from *Communication* by Barrie Hopson and Mike Scally; Times Publishing Group for the extract on p. 61 from *Culture Shock! Japan* by Rex Shelley, © Times Books International; 'Plague-free' and text no. 1 on p. 66 are reprinted by courtesy of the Cambridge Evening News; Reuters Ltd/The Guardian for text no. 2 p. 66; the text on p. 80 is adapted from *Urban Myths* by Phil Healey and Rick Glanvill, © 1992. Published by Virgin Publishing Ltd.; The Children's Society for exercise no. 3b on pp. 91 and 92 adapted from 'Divorce and You' leaflet in the Children's Society's *Divorce and You* pack, with permission; HarperCollins Publishers Ltd. for the extract on p. 92 from *Simon Mayo's Further Confessions*; Blackwell Publishers for exercises no. 2a, 2b and 2c adapted from *Intercultural Communication* by Ron Scollon and Suzanne Wong Scollon; the paragraphs 1, 3, 4 and 6 of exercice no. 3 on p. 95, are extracts from *Stipple, Wink and Gusset* by James Cochrane, reprinted by permission of Peter Fraser & Dunlop Group Ltd; Woody Allen for copyright material from *Manhattan* on p. 93.

The author and publishers are grateful to the following illustrators and photographic sources:

Illustrators: Andrew Davidson: p. 17; Ian Dicks: pp. 15, 33, 36, 37, 54 *l*, 77; Steve Gyapay: p. 7 *l*; Phil Healey: pp. 13, 38, 44, 47, 65, 70 *b*, 74; John Ireland: pp. 7 *r*, 51, 52, 54 *r*, 59, 60; Nicholas Martin: p. 68; Stephen May: pp. 6, 10, 18, 32, 34, 43, 48, 56, 63, 73; Lynne Russell: pp. 40, 76; Debbie Ryder: p. 14; Meilo So: pp. 19, 28, 69, 70 *t*; Kath Walker: pp. 24, 25, 45.

Cover illustration by Rosemary Woods.

Photographic sources: Art Directors Photo Library: pp. 19, 20; Camera Press/Walter Bennett: p. 28 *tr*; Mary Evans Picture Library: p. 24; Robert Harding Picture Library: pp. 48, 75; Hulton Deutsch Collection/ Sports Photo: pp. 28 *tl*; Hulton Deutsch Collection: pp. 68, 69; The Hutchison Library: p. 8 *cl*; Nigel Luckhurst: p. 36; The Mansell Collection: p. 72; Mike Goldwater/ Network Photographers: p. 8 *l*; Gideon Mendel/Network Photographers: p. 38; NSPCC (photo posed by model): p. 26; Panos/Dominic Sansoni: p. 8 *r*; Popperfoto: p. 28 *bl*; Rex Features Limited: p. 16 *t*, 28 *br*; Rex Features Limited/Chris Harris: p. 16 *b*; Frank Spooner Pictures/Gamma: pp. 30, 64, 66; Tony Stone Images/ Paul Morroll: p. 46; The Sunday Times, London/Jake Chessum: p. 22; Tropix/I. Sheldrick: p. 8 *cr*; United Artists (courtesy Kobal): p. 42.

All other photographs taken by Steve Bond at F64.

t = top   *b* = bottom   *c* = centre   *l* = left   *r* = right

Picture research by Sandie Huskinson-Rolfe of PHOTOSEEKERS.

Book design by QuintonWong.